With Love
Carol Fay
'Biscuit Lady'

Loveless
CAFE
A Nashville Tradition Since 1951

Mike Harris
General Manger
mike @ lovelesscafe.com

www.lovelesscafe.com

8400 Highway 100 • Nashville, TN 37221
P 615.646.9700 • F 615.646.1056
C 615.948.6236

Love To Jamie   April 23,
Love ~ Mom ~   2007

SOUTHERN COUNTRY COOKING

from

HOT BISCUITS, COUNTRY HAM

JANE & MICHAEL STERN

RUTLEDGE HILL PRESS

Nashville, Tennessee

A Division of Thomas Nelson Publishers

Since 1798

www.thomasnelson.com

Published by Rutledge Hill Press, a Division of Thomas
Nelson, Inc., P.O. Box 141000, Nashville, Tennessee, 37214.

Rutledge Hill Press books may be purchased in bulk for
educational, business, fundraising, or sales promotional use. For
information, please email
SpecialMarkets@ThomasNelson.com.

Library of Congress Cataloging-in-Publication Data

Stern, Michael, 1946-
    Southern country cooking from the Loveless Café / Jane
& Michael Stern.
        p. cm.
    Includes index.
    ISBN-10: 1-4016-0214-2 (hardcover)
    ISBN-13: 978-1-4016-0214-7 (hardcover)
    1. Loveless (Café) 2. Cookery, American—Southern
style. I. Stern, Jane. II. Title.
TX715.2.S68
641.5975—dc22   2004027355

Printed in the United States of America
06 07 08 09 10—11 10 9 8 7

To Chuck and Trisha Elcan who had the vision,
the generosity, and the trust to make the preservation
of the Loveless Motel and Cafe possible

Contents

Acknowledgments

We have always loved the Loveless Cafe not only for its delicious food, but for the people who have made it a beacon of southern hospitality. Former owner Donna McCabe had a way of making everybody feel welcome; and that convivial tradition is upheld in high style by new owner Tom Morales. Tom's energy and passion for good food infuses the cafe and made our time there a joy. We are also grateful to the other members of the Loveless team who make visiting feel like a family reunion—especially Angie Gore, Chandni Patel, and Jesse Goldstein, who facilitated this book getting done.

We thank Rutledge Hill Press for having made a reality of our dream of commemorating favorite restaurants around the country in a series of Roadfood cookbooks. In particular, we are grateful to Larry Stone, Pamela Clements, and Roger Waynick. Who make things happen. We also thank Geoff Stone for his scrupulous editing and Bryan Curtis for his good ideas to spread the word.

The friendship and guidance of our comrades at *Gourmet* magazine are a constant inspiration as we travel around the country researching our "Roadfood" column. Like many writers, we tend to write with particular readers in mind—readers who motivate us to do our best. In this case, Ruth Reichl, James Rodewald, Bill Sertl, Larry Karol, Shannon Fox, and "Doc" Willoughby are muses who are always at our side.

We never hit the road without our virtual companions at *www.roadfood.com*—Steve Rushmore Sr., Stephen Rushmore and Kristin Little, Cindy Keuchle, and Marc Bruno—who constantly fan the flames of appetite and discovery along America's highways and byways. As the web site has grown, we have found ourselves part of a great national community of people who love to travel and explore local foodways as much as we do. For the support and encouragement of all those who take part in the ongoing adventure of Roadfood.com, we are deeply obliged.

Thanks also to agent Doe Coover for her tireless work on our behalf, and to Jean Wagner, Jackie Willing, Mary Ann Rudolph, and Ned Schankman for making it possible for us to travel in confidence that all's well at home.

Foreword

Growing up in a large family, I look back now with the respect that only comes with age at how my mother was a short-order cook most of her adult life. It was my dad, though, who was always yelling for one of us ten siblings to start the grill and cook something. In other words, "Get your mom out of the kitchen." We learned things people pay culinary schools lots of money to learn, and, yet, they still may not learn the same thrifty style that we were taught as kids. We learned cooking techniques; we learned all the ways to use—and not to use—a knife; we learned ways to extend ingredients to feed more people. And we became experts on the grill. (I still say the true test of a chef is being able to take a cheap cut of meat and make it tasty. Face it, filet is easy.) The running joke in our family was that as much cooking as we did, one of us should be in the food business. I was the one whose life has been spent in the food service industry, owning a fine dining restaurant and a movie catering business. Still, it is the Loveless Motel and Cafe that has brought me full circle, that has, in a culinary sense, brought me back home.

Comfort food is the heart and soul of southern cuisine. It encompasses a time when people ate what was indigenous to the area in which they lived. Before the "super highways," the rural South was a remote area with back roads leading to treasures known only to those who ventured down them. For years the Loveless was one of those treasures, a place where Annie Loveless served fried chicken out the front door of her home. Those lucky enough to discover Annie and her husband Lon ate on picnic tables in their front yard. Return trips were planned around this stop, and lifelong rituals began.

The Loveless Cafe represents a time when people knew how to make red-eye gravy and scratch biscuits and took the time to do it. Back then, meals were the focal points for the day. Upcoming plans were discussed over a hearty breakfast. The noontime meal was fashioned around the previous night's leftovers, accompanied by iced tea. Supper was where we all got together to discuss our days—what went right and what went wrong. It was the highlight of the day, and Mama spent most of the afternoon preparing it. The food was not processed, an apple a day did keep the doctor away, and vegetables were the main staple. The ingredients were all local, usually from the farm or garden. Gardens were a ritual of rural life and what was planted was a science, ensuring produce from early spring until the last harvest in late fall.

Country hams were part of the fall harvest. They were cured to last without the luxury of freezers and without the need to feed the pigs through the winter. Cornbread and biscuits were fillers, and gravy was the sauce that made the meal complete. Hunting and fishing provided the variety. Folks remember those times when they come to the Loveless.

The Loveless is a cherished community asset that in today's fast-paced world could easily have been torn down to make room for another fast food joint. It is a treasure trove of memories "out Highway 100," and generations of families come back to relive those memories. Many who visit the Loveless for the first time are taken back to their own memories when life seemed slower, simpler, sweeter. The Loveless is so much more than a restaurant. It will survive.

In the pages of this cookbook are the stories, the pictures, and, most important, the recipes that make the South, southern cooking, and the Loveless special. If you can't make it to the north end of the Natchez Trace Parkway, you can now enjoy a bit of the Loveless in your own kitchen.

To my friends Chuck and Trisha, my wife Kathie and the staff that poured all their energy into this effort, thank you. To Jane and Michael Stern whose recognition that the Loveless truly is a jewel, thank you. To the families of the Lovelesses, the Maynards and the McCabes that came before us, thank you. This cookbook represents part of that tradition, enjoy!

— Tom Morales

Introduction

Eating at the Loveless Cafe isn't only a matter of fried chicken, country ham, and biscuits. It is all about the heart and soul of the South, Tennessee and Nashville in particular. As comfortable as an old rocking chair and as welcoming as grandma, the Loveless Cafe is a restaurant that resonates with country character. The curtains, made from antique linen tablecloths and old kitchen aprons, the bead board walls and red-checkered tablecloths, the innate hospitality of waitresses who have been a part of the place for decades are all facets of a restaurant that is so much more than a place to eat.

When we tucked into our first breakfast here in the 1970s, it was still pretty much a locals' place, as well as a favorite haunt of country musicians, famous and struggling, for whom its down-home meals were a touchstone of reality. At that time there was a newspaper clipping displayed on the wall headlined: "Funky Cafe Attracts Celebrities." And sure enough, out back in the parking lot we spotted a flashy private motor coach from which issued a troupe of well-known pickers and singers performing at Opryland. Inside, the famous customers were given no special treatment; like us, and like everyone else seated at the wobbly tables in the old dining room, they were made to feel as though they had come home for supper. Family-style platters of food were brought by waitresses who greeted all with smiles and consideration.

Even if it wasn't yet the far-famed landmark it has become, the Loveless Cafe could get crowded twenty-some years ago. If you knew you were coming during peak mealtime, you would need to call and make a reservation, and when you called, you would have to tell them whether you were planning on having fried chicken or country ham. That was pretty much the extent of the menu, along with the mainstay companions: biscuits, cream gravy, red-eye gravy, peach preserves, blackberry preserves, honey, and sorghum syrup. Now the kitchen's reper-

toire has grown—although country ham and fried chicken remain the anchor meals—and the Loveless Cafe has itself become a national celebrity. Among the luminaries who have visited in recent years are Britain's Princess Anne (in the neighborhood for a horse show), Paul McCartney (who spontaneously sang "Happy Birthday" to a sixteen-year-old customer who had come to celebrate with friends), Martha Stewart (who declared it "the best breakfast I've ever had"), and NBC's Willard Scott (who saluted the "World's Greatest Scratch Biscuits").

Despite its esteemed reputation, the Loveless Cafe remains faithful to its roots, and like a true-hearted singing star who hits the big-time, it has never strayed from the fundamental good things that led to its original success. First among them is fried chicken . . . the original meal served by Lon and Annie Loveless back in the early 1950s when they began offering picnic suppers to

Celebrity fans of the Loveless Cafe plaster the walls

passers-by along Highway 100. Customers got their food and ate it at picnic tables in the front yard. Along with chicken, of course, there is country ham. (Back in the late 1980s, after the motel adjoining the cafe was shuttered, a couple of the old rooms were used to hang hams as they aged. We poked our heads into one of those rooms one day: what an unforgettable aroma!)

Biscuits have always been essential to the culinary identity of the Loveless, and the recipe for the ones you eat today is essentially the same as that originally used by Annie Loveless. It was passed along to the next owners, Cordell and Stella Maynard, then to Donna McCabe, whose chief biscuit maker, Carol Fay Ellison, still mixes, rolls, and cuts them every day. Along with the biscuits, the time-honored Loveless meal always includes homemade preserves: amber peach and sultry blackberry go back to the beginnings, and strawberry joined the roster several years ago. Sorghum from west Tennessee and honey from local combs complete the biscuit service.

Delicious food is its main attraction, especially to travelers in search of a distinctive regional meal, but for citizens of central Tennessee the Loveless Cafe is also part of everyday life. Even those who don't eat here several times a week come to the Loveless on a regular basis to meet friends over the sociable meals turned out by this kitchen. It is remarkable how many old-time customers tell stories about visiting the Loveless years ago with their family for weekend get-togethers (which always included swimming in the nearby Harpeth River). "There is a valuable place in so many people's lives created here at the Loveless," owner Tom Morales says. "They came here to celebrate birthdays and anniversaries or to join with their families for Sunday supper. As I see it, the Loveless has unique status as a one-of-a-kind slice of Tennessee history. There's no place else like it in the world."

Loveless Cafe & Motel

Nashville is a city of legends. The story of the Loveless Cafe is one of them. Starting as a humble family home in a place that was far out in the country a century ago, it became the Harpeth Valley Tea Room in 1951 when it was bought by Lon and Annie Loveless of nearby Hickman County (where Lon had been sheriff). The couple had opened a restaurant over in Lyles back in 1936—The Beacon Light Tea Room— and they began in their new place west of Nashville as a kind of ad hoc food stand. They sold chicken out the front door to travelers who ate at picnic tables in the front yard. Business was good, and they decided to expand. The interior of the family home was transformed into a dining room and kitchen, and their tea room soon sported a menu almost identical to that still served today at the Beacon Light some forty miles west: ham, fried chicken, biscuits, and all the trimmings.

The cafe was adjoined by a small motel that became the domain of Lon Loveless, who, despite his surname, is said to have cultivated its reputation as a lovers' rendezvous. Garage doors were built in on either side so guests could park their cars out of sight. Even before its stint as a no-tell motel, this property was known as a place to go at least a little wild. As a private home having one of the largest hardwood living room floors around, it was a 1940s party house. "We danced till the walls shook!" recalled one woman who revisited the Loveless Cafe during its reopening week in 2004. "I learned to jitterbug right here."

The restaurant reflected the taste and talents of Annie Loveless. Her biscuits and homemade jams began to earn her a sterling reputation among Nashville families as well as among travelers heading out of town towards Memphis who were lucky enough to discover the cafe. Locals made the Loveless a destination dining spot for weekend suppers, and stars of the Grand Ole Opry drove out from Music City to become devoted fans. As roads improved and Nashville grew, the Loveless Cafe no longer seemed such a distant destination, but it maintained its low-key country personality: simple menu, friendly staff, modest prices, and endless supplies of hot biscuits throughout the meal.

In 1959, Cordell and Stella Maynard bought the Loveless Cafe along with Annie's biscuit recipe. They maintained its menu and its spirit; then in 1973, the place was bought by Charles and Donna McCabe. Their son George, then twelve, worked alongside his parents at the soon-to-be-famous cafe and became partners with his mother in 1982 when his father passed away. It was in the 1970s and 1980s that the modest road-side eatery that once had been Nashville's secret went national. Discovered by food writers and featured on national television shows, the Loveless found itself recognized as a precious cultural institution.

It is no coincidence that its rise to prominence occurred exactly when the fast food industry in America was burgeoning. As corporate sameness spread alongside highways throughout the land, restaurants with individual regional character became all the more precious to those who felt strongly about old fashioned values, culinary and other-wise. With its traditional menu, personality-plus waitresses, and rural charm, the Loveless was something much more valuable than a good place to eat. For us, when we wrote the first edition of Roadfood in the mid-1970s, a meal at this friendly cafe symbolized everything we hold dear about American regional food.

Beseeched by out-of-towners who got a taste for the country ham and preserves and wanted more, George McCabe started Loveless Motel & Cafe Hams & Jams in the mid-1980s, offering whole Tennessee hams, center-cut slices, homemade preserves, smoked sausage and bacon, sorghum, and honey. The business is still thriving and now fea-tures breakfast gift packs with everything but hot biscuits.

At the beginning of the new century, Donna McCabe was looking to retire. "I knew I'd never get her to quit working as long as we owned it," her son George said, adding, "It was time for the Loveless to undergo renovation and expansion." When Tom Morales agreed to buy it, McCabe was thrilled. "We looked for someone to take it over who would maintain what's great and unique about the Loveless, and who would have the resources to make the necessary improvements. We're happy to say we've found the right person to carry on the Loveless tradition, and we're thrilled that it's someone from Nashville who knows the cafe's his-tory and wants to hold onto its legacy for future generations."

That is exactly how Tom Morales sees his job. "People go to the

Loveless Motel & Cafe because it allows them to step back in time," he says. "As fast-paced as our world is today, people don't have time to make biscuits from scratch, to make their own preserves, or to make red-eye gravy. But they like a place where they can get those things and get them as they were passed down from generation to generation. The Loveless offers an authentic experience that reminds people of their childhood and of great southern traditions."

Drinks

Iced Tea

Fruited Peach Tea

Homemade Lemonade

Watermelon Punch

ICED TEA

Known as the "champagne of the South," sweet tea is an essential part of meals in cafes and in homes. "It's not just the sugar that makes ice tea southern," Tom Morales notes. "It's the way you say sweet *tay*."

6	cups water
6	tea bags (standard size)
6	to 8 tablespoons sugar
10	fresh mint leaves (optional)

Bring the water to a boil. Put the tea bags in the water and let them steep for 10 minutes. Strain the tea into a large pitcher and add the sugar and mint leaves. Fill the pitcher with ice and serve.

MAKES 4 TO 6 SERVINGS

FRUITED PEACH TEA

Tom says that sweet tea is such a staple on the table, especially in the summer, that a variation is often welcome. "Long hot days drinking lots of sweet tea motivated this simple twist for something different and equally refreshing."

3	tea bags
6	cups boiling water
4	cups peach nectar
1	bunch mint leaves
2	lemons, sliced

Brew the tea bags in the boiling water to make a strong tea. Refrigerate until chilled. Mix the tea with the peach nectar in a large pitcher and add the mint leaves and lemon slices. Let the tea stand for 30 minutes to 1 hour.

MAKES 8 TO 12 SERVINGS

HOMEMADE LEMONADE

Lemonade is nearly as popular in the South as tea. "As much as I like lemonade, my favorite way to have it is half-and-half with tea," Tom notes. He adds that he tends to make his by the glass, rather than in batches.

2	*cups sugar*
½	*cup fresh squeezed lemon juice*
¼	*teaspoon salt*
8	*cups water*
2	*lemons, thinly sliced*

Put the sugar, lemon juice, salt, and water into the pitcher. Stir well until the sugar is dissolved. Add the lemon slices.

MAKES 8 TO 12 SERVINGS

Variations: For ginger lemonade, peel a small knob (2 ounces) of ginger and cut into 3 or 4 slices. Bring 1 cup of water to a boil and let the ginger steep in the water with ¼ cup sugar for 10 minutes. Remove the ginger slices and add the flavored sugar-water to the lemonade. Serve chilled.

WATERMELON PUNCH

Watermelon punch is fine by itself," Tom allows. But he adds with a chuckle that the motivation for making this punch is usually to spike it. "Vodka, tequila, any basic clear liquor works, even rum."

1	large watermelon (about 10 pounds), refrigerated
	Sugar
⅛	teaspoon salt
1	(8-ounce) can orange juice concentrate
2	cups crushed ice
1	to 2 cups vodka or white rum (optional)

Cut the watermelon in half, scoop out the fruit, and put it in a bowl. Squish the melon with both hands and break it up into pulp. Strain with a large sieve and extract the juice. Add the sugar to taste, then salt, and then the orange juice concentrate. Grind the ice in a blender with the watermelon juice. Stir in the vodka or rum if desired.

MAKES 10 TO 12 SERVINGS

Breakfasts & Breads

Falls Mills White Corn Grits

Hoe Cakes

Barbecue Breakfast & Hoe Cakes

Baked Pancake Casserole

Corn Muffins

Corn Fritters

Granola

Eggs Loveless with Tomato Gravy

Southern Omelet

"Egg in a House"

Candied Bacon

Hashbrown Casserole

Sausage Suzanne Brunch Casserole

Ham & Egg Casserole

Chicken Hash

Hot Pineapple

Peach Scones

Sour Cream Coffee Cake

Blueberry Muffins

Strawberry Muffins

Banana Bread

Easy Banana Muffins

Country Ham Spoon Bread

Aunt Kat's Spoon Bread

Heavenly Cornbread

FALLS MILLS WHITE CORN GRITS

Loveless grits are ground at a Tennessee water-powered gristmill that has been in operation since 1873.

1	cup grits
1	tablespoon butter
½	teaspoon salt
	Black pepper

Put the grits in a saucepan, cover with water, and stir. Light bran will float to the top. Pour off the water and bran and then place 2 cups of water, the butter, and salt in saucepan and bring the mixture to a boil. Reduce the heat to low and cook covered for 20 minutes, stirring until rich and creamy. Season with black pepper to taste.

MAKES 4 SERVINGS

Note: You may add cream, cheese, or sugar. Serve hot.

Carol Fay Ellison

Carol Fay Ellison is the steady anchor in the kitchen of the Loveless Cafe. Business tides may ebb and flow, but her biscuits are a constant fact of life, as are the fruit preserves she makes to go with them.

One of ten children who grew up in a home where Mother made biscuits for the family, Carol Fay started work as a dish-washer at the Loveless twenty-six years ago. One day when some-one didn't come in for work, she filled in as a line cook making eggs, ham, and sausage. "Oh, lordy, it was hot then," she remembers. "If it was a hundred degrees outside, it was two hun-dred in the kitchen. You had to walk into the freezer to get cool."

Gifted with expertise learned from watching her mother, she soon became the biscuit lady. Biscuits had always been an essential part of the cafe's meals; when they became her responsibility, she made a change or two in the recipe and created what has since become a Loveless signature. "They had been using powdered milk, buttermilk, and water," she recalls. "But with powdered milk, you make a dough that chunks and gunks. So I took it out of the recipe." Precious few people have since apprenticed with Carol Fay to become proficient as biscuit makers. "It can be tough teaching people," she says. "A lot of them don't want to put their fingers in the dough. And handling the dough just right is key."

As she describes it, making preserves is a less exacting science. "All I do is add sugar to the fruit," she reveals. "We used to cook them on the stove in big old rondos. Now I've got a tilt skillet, and we make preserves every day."

After the Loveless shut down for remodeling early in 2004, Carol Fay's skills and experience were key ingredients in a new kitchen that would stay true to the cafe's culinary roots. "When we reopened, I did 149 hours in the first two weeks," she says with a serene smile.

Jesse Goldstein, vice-president of operations for TomKats, the company that saved and revived the Loveless Cafe, told us that Carol Fay's presence in the new kitchen is essential, and not only because she is keeper of the precious biscuit recipe. As one who has been an essential part of the Loveless Cafe for more than a quarter century, she embodies an indomitable spirit that gives strength to those around her. "I love her," Jesse says. "There is no one in the world better to hug, or to be hugged by."

HOE CAKES

A favorite bread of country folks in the South, hoe cakes are great under pulled pork barbecue with a side of coleslaw.

1½	cups cornmeal		1	egg, lightly beaten
¼	teaspoon baking soda		⅓	cup shortening or canola oil
1¼	cups buttermilk			

Combine the cornmeal and baking soda in a bowl. Stir in the buttermilk and beaten egg. Heat the oil in a skillet over medium-high heat. Pour ½ cup batter into the skillet. Fry until golden brown on both sides. Repeat with remaining batter.

MAKES 4 TO 6 SERVINGS (2 CUPS)

BARBECUE BREAKFAST & HOE CAKES

Tom ate barbecue on hoecakes when he was growing up, but this particular recipe reminds him of a breakfast place in Fort Walton Beach, Florida, where he used to joke with the waitress to give him one egg to the left and one egg to the right. And that's just how he got them!

½	cup canola oil		1	pound Pulled Pork (see page 108)
1	cup shoe peg corn			
2	cups hoe cake mix (1 recipe above)		1	cup Loveless Barbecue Sauce (see page 80)
8	eggs			

Pour the oil into a skillet to cover the bottom. Heat the oil over medium-high heat. In a bowl combine the corn and hoe cake mix. When hot, ladle the mix into the oil. Brown the cakes on both sides and repeat to make eight cakes.

Cook the eggs to order. Place ¼ pound pork on top of hoe cakes and drizzle with ¼ cup of the sauce. Serve 2 hoe cakes and 2 eggs per serving.

MAKES 4 SERVINGS

BAKED PANCAKE CASSEROLE

Delicious with fruit and syrup or yogurt.

4	tablespoons butter
6	eggs
1	cup pancake mix
1	cup milk
1	teaspoon salt

Preheat the oven to 450°F. Melt the butter in a 9 x 13-inch baking dish in the oven. Combine the eggs, pancake mix, milk, and salt and pour the mixture into the dish. Bake for 25 to 30 minutes or until the top puffs up.

MAKES 8 TO 10 SERVINGS

CORN MUFFINS

Skillet-cooked cornbread is the everyday way; using cast-iron molds to make cornbread muffins is more for Sunday supper or special-occasion meals.

¾	cup cornmeal		2	eggs, beaten
½	teaspoon salt		1	teaspoon baking powder
¾	cup boiling water		2	tablespoons butter, melted
½	cup milk			

Preheat the oven to 425°F. Sift the cornmeal and salt into a small bowl. Pour in the boiling water and mix well. Add the milk and mix well. Stir in the beaten eggs, baking powder, and butter and mix well. Spoon into eight large, nonstick muffin cups. Bake for 20 to 25 minutes or until brown.

MAKES 8 SERVINGS

CORN FRITTERS

Corn has always been a staple in the southern kitchen," Tom reminds us. "Spoon bread, muffins, and hoe cakes are all variations of the same idea. A fritter is the deep-fried version."

3½	cups sifted all-purpose flour
1	teaspoon baking powder
6	egg yolks
½	cup milk
½	cup sugar
½	teaspoon salt
24	ounces frozen corn kernels, thawed and drained
6	egg whites
	Oil, as needed

Sift the flour with the baking powder in a large bowl. Make a well in the center. In a separate bowl mix together the egg yolks, milk, sugar, and salt. Add to the flour, pouring the wet mixture into the well. Blend together until smooth. Add the corn to the mixture and blend well. In a chilled bowl beat the egg whites until stiff. Gently fold them into the corn mixture and incorporate. Heat the oil in deep skillet or fryer, and drop the batter into the oil using a portion scoop. Place on paper towels to drain. May be served with syrup or confectioners' sugar.

MAKES 10 TO 12 SERVINGS

GRANOLA

When the Loveless reopened at the beginning of 2004, it was felt that granola would be a good recipe to add to the menu especially for all the tourists on bicycles who ride by. This recipe is based on one Alisa Huntsman developed years ago in San Francisco, but here sorghum complements the honey.

1	cup plus 2 tablespoons firmly packed brown sugar
4	cups roughly chopped pecans
10½	cups whole rolled oats (do not use instant oats)
1	tablespoon ground cinnamon
3	ounces (6 tablespoons) sorghum
3	ounces (6 tablespoons) honey
1	pound unsalted butter

Preheat the oven to 350°F. Toss together the brown sugar, pecans, rolled oats, and cinnamon. Be sure to break up all of the sugar lumps and to mix it in well. In a small saucepan melt together the sorghum, honey, and butter. Pour this mix over the oat mix and combine thoroughly. Pour into a large cake pan or roasting pan with at least 2-inch sides. Be sure to spray the pan with nonstick cooking spray first. Bake for 45 minutes to 1 hour. Every 10 to 15 minutes, remove the pan from the oven and stir completely. Do this until the mix is evenly toasted. Cool completely before storing. Be sure to store it in an absolutely airtight container or it will become soggy.

MAKES ABOUT 16 CUPS

Note: If desired, substitute honey, light molasses, or maple syrup for the sorghum.

EGGS LOVELESS WITH TOMATO GRAVY

Tom Morales practically breaks out into song when he rhapsodizes about the goodness of the grits cakes that are the foundation of this gloss on Eggs Benedict. "What we do at the end of the day is take the grits we haven't used, add some Parmesan cheese to thicken them up, add a little flavor, and then lay them out on a sheet pan to cool overnight. In the morning, we take a big biscuit cutter and cut the grits into rounds, which are then floured and fried. You place these grits cakes on a plate with pieces of country ham and eggs-over-easy. Then top it with tomato gravy. Awesome!"

Grits cakes

1	recipe grits (see page 13)
¼	cup Parmesan cheese
1	tablespoon salt
1	tablespoon pepper
½	cup all-purpose flour
½	cup canola oil

Tomato gravy

½	cup bacon grease (or ¼ cup canola oil and ¼ cup country ham drippings)
2	tablespoons all-purpose flour
1	cup milk
1	(12-ounce) can chopped tomatoes (or 12 peeled, seeded, and chopped fresh tomatoes)
	Salt and pepper
8	(2-ounce) portions country ham, cooked in a skillet
8	eggs, fried

Take the grits after they have cooled and thickened and mix in the Parmesan cheese. Spread the mixture on a large baking sheet. Take a large biscuit or cookie cutter and cut out the grit mix. Add the salt, pepper, and flour together in a small plastic bag. Shake thoroughly and pour onto a plate. Press the grits cakes into the flour to coat both sides. In a skillet over medium heat add the oil to cover the bottom. When the oil is hot but not smoking, drop in the grits cakes, browning both sides. Remove and reserve.

For the tomato gravy, put the bacon grease in a skillet over medium-high heat. Add the flour and stir until well mixed. Add the milk and stir until it boils. Add the tomatoes and return to a boil. Add the salt and pepper to taste. If too thick, add water and stir.

Place two cooked grits cakes on a plate. Place a country ham portion on top of each. Place a fried egg on top of the ham on each grits cake. Ladle the tomato gravy over the top and enjoy.

MAKES 4 TO 6 SERVINGS

SOUTHERN OMELET

A Tennessee twist on the traditional western omelet, here made with country ham or Loveless sausage or bacon.

2	tablespoons diced yellow onion		3	eggs
2	tablespoons diced green pepper		¾	cup shredded Cheddar cheese
¼	pound ham, bacon, or sausage, chopped			

Place two skillets over medium heat. In one skillet sauté the onion, pepper, and meat. Add the eggs to the other skillet, breaking the yolks. When the eggs start to harden, flip them over and add the onion, peppers, and meats on top of egg. Add the cheese, roll the omelet out onto a plate, and serve.

MAKES 1 OMELET

"EGG IN A HOUSE"

Tom suggests this amusing presentation is especially good for children who don't want to eat their eggs in the morning.

2	slices white or wheat bread		2	eggs
¼	pound (1 stick) butter			Salt and pepper

Take a cookie cutter and core the middle of each slice of bread. Melt the butter and brush both sides of the bread slices with the butter. Heat a skillet over medium heat and place the bread in the hot skillet. Pour the remaining butter equally in the bread holes. Crack an egg in each bread hole. When the egg starts to harden and the bread browns, flip and continue to cook until the opposite side is browned or eggs are done to your liking. Add salt and pepper to taste.

MAKES 2 SERVINGS

CANDIED BACON

A great way to beat the ho-hum, and an especially appreciated touch for a BLT.

⅓   cup light brown sugar
½   teaspoon ground cumin
8   slices bacon

Preheat the oven to 400°F. Mix the brown sugar and cumin. Dredge the bacon on both sides in the sugar mixture. Place the bacon on a baking pan with sides and bake for 15 to 20 minutes or until brown. Place on a paper towel to drain the excess fat. Serve warm.

MAKES 4 SERVINGS

HASHBROWN CASSEROLE

This recipe made it to the Loveless back in the 1950s when canned-soup cookery was at its peak. It has since become a favorite side dish among regular customers.

1   (30-ounce) bag shredded hash brown potatoes
1   yellow onion, chopped
1   (8-ounce) bag shredded Cheddar cheese
1   (10¾-ounce) can cream of chicken soup
1   (16-ounce) container sour cream
1   tablespoon salt
1   tablespoon black pepper

Preheat the oven to 375°F. Combine the potatoes, onion, cheese, soup, sour cream, salt and pepper. Mix well, pour into a 9 x 13-inch greased casserole dish, and bake for 25 to 30 minutes or until the top is browned.

MAKES 6 TO 8 SERVINGS

SAUSAGE SUZANNE BRUNCH CASSEROLE

Here's a casserole that can be made the day before and heated for brunch. Tom calls it a "no-worry, no stress recipe passed down from my partner's mom."

½	pound mild sausage
4	slices bread with crusts trimmed
4	eggs, beaten
1	cup milk
1	teaspoon dry mustard
1	teaspoon salt
2	cups shredded Cheddar cheese

Brown the sausage in a skillet, stirring until crumbly and cooked through; drain. Tear the bread into bite-size pieces. Combine the sausage, bread, eggs, milk, dry mustard, salt, and cheese in a bowl; mix well. Pour into a 2-quart nonstick casserole. Chill, covered, for 8 to 10 hours. Bake at 325°F for 50 minutes.

MAKES 7 TO 8 SERVINGS

HAM & EGG CASSEROLE

This can be made ahead and served side by side with another casserole. Tom recalls that casseroles were especially popular for after-church or after-baptism parties because they could be heated and served quickly, without having to risk cooking in your good clothes. He suggests serving it with fresh fruit and an assortment of hot sauces.

2	cups chopped ham
4	hard-boiled eggs, sliced
1	(4-ounce) can sliced mushrooms, drained
1	(10-ounce) can cream of mushroom soup
1	(10-ounce) can cream of celery soup
½	to 1 soup can milk
8	ounces medium Cheddar cheese, shredded

Preheat the oven to 350°F. Layer the ham, eggs, and mushrooms in a 2-quart casserole. Combine the soups and milk and pour over the top. Sprinkle with the cheese and bake until bubbly and the cheese is melted, about 15 minutes.

MAKES 4 TO 6 SERVINGS

Note: You can substitute mushroom pieces and stems for the sliced mushrooms.

CHICKEN HASH

So much good southern cooking comes from the necessity of stretching ingredients to make the most of them. Chicken hash is an opportunity to use every scrap.

"It's like hog's-head hash," Tom explains. "You use everything leftover from the hog you haven't eaten. This goes back to the days when there wasn't abundance." He recommends serving chicken hash for breakfast, lunch, or dinner.

1	cup cubed potatoes
1	cup chicken stock
½	cup diced onion
½	cup small-diced celery
½	tablespoon chopped garlic
2	tablespoons butter
	Salt and pepper
¼	cup fresh herbs (thyme, rosemary, parsley)
1	cup cubed cooked chicken
2	tablespoons heavy cream

Blanch the potatoes with salt to taste in the chicken stock. Cook until the potatoes are done. In a medium skillet over medium heat, sauté the onions, celery, and garlic in the butter. Add salt and pepper to taste. Add the fresh herbs, potatoes, and chicken. Finish with the heavy cream. Serve over cornbread waffles and with over-easy or over-medium eggs on top.

MAKES 4 SERVINGS

HOT PINEAPPLE

Great for brunch.

1	(20-ounce) can pineapple chunks, drained, but with some juice
1	(16-ounce) can crushed pineapple, drained
1	cup grated Cheddar cheese
½	cup sugar
3	tablespoons all-purpose flour
4	tablespoons pineapple juice
½	cup (1 stick) butter
1	sleeve Ritz crackers, crushed

Preheat the oven to 350°F. Put the pineapple in a 1-quart casserole dish with the cheese. Mix together the sugar, flour, and pineapple juice. Blend well. Pour over the pineapple. In a skillet melt the butter and add the crushed crackers. Stir until the butter is absorbed and the cracker crumbs are coated. Pour the cracker mix on top of the pineapple mixture. Bake for 30 minutes.

MAKES 4 TO 6 SERVINGS

PEACH SCONES

I get a lot of people telling me that these are not real scones," Alisa Huntsman told us. "They say real scones have to have cream or eggs. But I believe that a scone recipe is like a curry recipe: every family has its favorite way of doing it. This one is not sweet, and you can add spices, fresh or frozen fruit, or chocolate chips."

2	cups unbleached all-purpose flour
3	tablespoons sugar plus some for sprinkling
¼	teaspoon salt
2	teaspoons baking powder
½	teaspoon ginger
½	teaspoon ground cinnamon
½	cup (1 stick) cold, unsalted butter, cut into cubes
½	cup dried peaches, diced
⅔	cup buttermilk

Preheat the oven to 400°F. Sift together the flour, 3 tablespoons sugar, salt, baking powder, ginger, and cinnamon in a bowl. Stir to incorporate. Cut the butter into the flour mix until the size of small peas, using a pastry cutter or two butter knives. (If you have a food processor, place all of the dry ingredients in the processor bowl without sifting them. Add the butter and pulse until the butter is pea size.) In a mixing bowl, stir the peaches into the flour-butter mix. Add the buttermilk and gently mix together until a ball is formed. On a floured surface, pat out the dough into a 7-inch round disk. Cut into eight wedges. Place on a baking sheet lined with parchment paper and sprinkle with the remaining sugar. Bake for 15 to 20 minutes or until golden around the edges and on the bottom.

MAKES 8 SERVINGS

SOUR CREAM COFFEE CAKE

When asked why he likes this recipe so much, Tom declared, "Not all breakfast has to be fried!"

½	cup softened margarine
1	cup sugar
1	teaspoon vanilla extract
2	eggs
2	cups plus 3 tablespoons all-purpose flour
1	teaspoon baking powder
1	teaspoon baking soda
1	teaspoon salt
1	cup sour cream
3	tablespoons margarine, melted
¾	cup packed brown sugar
2	teaspoons ground cinnamon
¾	cup chopped nuts (walnuts or pecans)

Cream the softened margarine and the sugar in a mixer bowl until light and fluffy. Beat in the vanilla and eggs. Combine the 2 cups flour, baking powder, baking soda, and salt and sift over the egg mixture alternately with the sour cream, mixing well after each addition. Pour half the batter into a greased and floured 9 x 13-inch baking pan. Preheat the oven to 350°F. Combine the 3 tablespoons flour, melted margarine, brown sugar, cinnamon, and nuts in a small bowl; mix well. Sprinkle half the brown sugar mixture over the batter in the pan. Spread the remaining batter over the top. Sprinkle with the remaining brown sugar mixture. Bake for 25 to 30 minutes or until light brown.

MAKES 10 SERVINGS

BLUEBERRY MUFFINS

Pastry chef Alisa Huntsman loves this recipe because it is so versatile. It can be used for muffins or cakes and can incorporate all kinds of fruits or chocolate chips. "So many places use mixes for their muffins," she said. "But I refuse to use mix."

½	cup (1 stick) unsalted butter, melted and cooled
1¼	cups sugar
¼	teaspoon salt
2	large eggs at room temperature
1	teaspoon vanilla extract
2	to 2⅓ cups unbleached all-purpose flour
2	teaspoons baking powder
1	cup blueberries (fresh or frozen)
½	cup buttermilk

Preheat the oven to 375°F. Whisk the butter, sugar, salt, eggs, and vanilla together in a bowl. Sift the flour and baking powder over the butter mix. Add the berries to the flour mix and gently fold a few times. Add the buttermilk and gently mix together. Scoop out the dough into paper-lined muffin pans. Will make six Texas-size muffins or twelve standard muffins. Sprinkle with additional sugar and bake 20 to 35 minutes, depending on the size of the muffins.

MAKES 6 LARGE OR 12 SMALL MUFFINS

STRAWBERRY MUFFINS

This is a variation of the Blueberry Muffins but for strawberry lovers.

½	cup (1 stick) unsalted butter, melted and cooled
1¼	plus ¼ cups sugar
¼	teaspoon salt
2	large eggs at room temperature
1	teaspoon vanilla extract
	Zest of ½ orange
2⅓	cups unbleached all-purpose flour
2	teaspoons baking powder
¼	teaspoon nutmeg
2	tablespoons plus ½ teaspoon cinnamon
1	cup roughly chopped strawberries (fresh or frozen)
½	cup buttermilk

Preheat the oven to 375°F. Whisk the butter, 1¼ cups sugar, salt, eggs, vanilla, and orange zest together in a bowl. Sift the flour, baking powder, nutmeg, and ½ teaspoon cinnamon over the butter mix. Add the berries to the flour mix and gently fold a few times. Add the buttermilk and gently mix together. Scoop out the dough into paper-lined muffin pans. Will make six Texas-size muffins or twelve standard muffins. Combine the remaining 2 tablespoons cinnamon with the remaining ¼ cup sugar and sprinkle on top of the muffins. Bake for 20 to 35 minutes, depending on the size of the muffins.

MAKES 6 LARGE OR 12 SMALL MUFFINS

BANANA BREAD

Who doesn't find themselves with a last banana from a bunch, too ripe for eating? Alisa's trick is to throw these leftovers in the freezer and, when she has enough, take them out to make banana bread. "They are very unappealing," she warns. "All black and liquid; but they are great for baking." This recipe creates what many southerners know as "tea bread," listed on the Loveless menu as "breakfast bread."

¼	pound (1 stick) unsalted butter, softened
1	cup sugar
2	large eggs at room temperature
1	cup sour cream
1	cup mashed bananas
2	cups unbleached all-purpose flour
1	teaspoon baking soda
1½	teaspoons ground cinnamon
½	cup walnut pieces

Preheat the oven to 350°F. Cream together the butter and sugar until light and fluffy. Add the eggs to the butter mix one at a time. Mix in well. Add the sour cream and bananas and stir until partially incorporated. Sift the flour, baking soda, and cinnamon over the batter and fold in gently. Add the walnuts and fold in gently. Pour into loaf pans that have been greased and floured. Bake for 25 to 35 minutes for mini loaves or 45 to 50 minutes for large loaves, or until a toothpick that is inserted comes out clean. Baking times will vary according to pan size.

MAKES 3 MINI LOAVES OR 1 LARGE LOAF

Variation: Substitute pumpkin purée for the bananas and use 1½ teaspoons pumpkin pie spice instead of the cinnamon.

EASY BANANA MUFFINS

The name of this recipe is no lie. Turn on the oven, martial the ingredients, and within minutes, baking muffins will be perfuming the kitchen.

3	*large bananas*
¾	*cup sugar*
1	*egg, beaten*
⅓	*cup butter, melted*
1	*teaspoon baking soda*
1	*teaspoon baking powder*
½	*teaspoon salt*
1½	*cups all-purpose flour*
1	*teaspoon vanilla extract*

Preheat the oven to 375°F. Mash the bananas in a large bowl. Add the sugar and egg. Add the butter and then the baking soda, baking powder, salt, and flour. Mix well and add the vanilla. Pour the batter into muffin tins and bake for 20 to 25 minutes.

MAKES 12 REGULAR MUFFINS

COUNTRY HAM SPOON BREAD

Ham bits make spoon bread taste great," Tom says about this dish that is pudding-like in its consistency.

4	cups chicken stock	2	egg yolks
1	cup whole milk	1	egg
1	cup heavy cream	4	ears corn, kernels cut off cob
¼	cup sugar	1	cup diced ham
1	cup half-and-half	1	cup grated Cheddar cheese
1	tablespoon salt	1	tablespoon flat-leaf parsley
1½	cups cornmeal	1	cup sliced scallions
2	egg whites, reserve yolks		Black pepper
1	teaspoon baking powder		Worcestershire sauce
¼	pound (1 stick) butter		Hot sauce

Grease a 10 x 12-inch baking tray with vegetable spray. Preheat a convection oven to 375°F (400°F for conventional oven). In a saucepan, bring the chicken stock, milk, cream, sugar, and half-and-half to a simmer. Pour the salt and cornmeal into the mixture and stir well. Bring to a simmer again and reduce the heat. Whip the egg whites to soft peaks and add the baking powder. Fold the butter, egg yolks, egg, corn, ham, cheese, parsley, and scallions into the cornmeal mixture. Add the egg whites. Add ingredients in slowly. Add the black pepper, Worcestershire sauce, and hot sauce to taste. Pour the mixture into the pan and bake for 30 minutes uncovered. Cover with aluminum foil and cook 30 minutes at 300°F or until set.

MAKES 12 TO 15 SERVINGS

Country Ham

Country ham and ordinary ham are about as different as champagne and grape juice. If you've never had country ham, a first taste can be shocking. It has a pungent aroma; it is extremely salty; and it isn't all that tender. The really good whole ones that they sell at the Hams & Jams Country Market adjacent to the Loveless Cafe cost three times as much as the canned ones in a supermarket, and they come packaged in a burlap sack.

Ham has always been a star attraction of the Loveless menu. Waitress Marie Barrett says she occasionally gets a new customer who asks for ordinary ham because country ham is too salty. She advises such people to give ham at the Loveless a try. The smoke-cured hams of Tennessee are considerably less salty than those cured farther east in Virginia (which many consumers soak in tubs of water before cooking, just to draw out the salt); while Tennessee ham packs a tidal wave of profound, chewy character, the subtle complexities of its long-cured flavor are never overwhelmed by brackishness.

Wild and forceful though it may be, country ham is among the most tenderly nurtured of foods. Its muscular salty punch leads your tongue

towards a complex piquancy that speaks of a long curing process. Like veined cheese, sourdough bread, and vintage wine, great country ham awakens that special fascination taste buds have for flavors that teeter on the refined side of rot.

Traditionally, the making of a country ham begins in the fall. The hind leg of a freshly-butchered hog is rubbed with salt, sometimes sugar or pepper, as well as sodium nitrate or nitrite to improve color and to resist spoilage. The curing "green ham" absorbs its spice rub in a cool, dark storage area over a course of about four weeks, during which time it weeps moisture. After a month of losing water weight, a ham is washed, strung up in a net bag, and aged several more months. During that time, it develops a veil of mold, it sheds more weight, its flesh tightens, and its flavor grows ever more intense. Traditional producers age hams a minimum of six months, and some will keep a few special ones hung up for years. To connoisseurs, the older the ham, the finer its character.

As a ham hangs through the winter and into spring, a Tennessee ham house wafts hickory smoke into the aging barn. Originally, this began as a practical solution for the fly problem, but today the insinuation of sweet wood flavor from the smoke house is a fundamental part of many hams' characters.

It's heaven to eat ham at a table in the Loveless Cafe—either served on a plate with eggs and hash brown casserole or sandwiched in warm buttermilk biscuits. But even if you can't come to the Loveless, it's a special treat to order one by mail. Large, odd-shaped, and heavy as wet clay, it defies disguise in any ordinary container.

Cooking a whole country ham can seem like a daunting task, but in truth the biggest challenge is finding a pan big enough to hold it. The one tragic mistake a ham novice can make is to unwrap the costly prize, look at its ugly coat of mold and perhaps pepper that resembles dirt, and determine that it is spoiled. It is not! Mold is a natural part of the ham-curing process, and it should be scraped off with a stiff brush under a stream of cool water. Next, soak the ham a full day in tap water. (If you need it to be less salty, change the water a few times.) Cooking is simply a matter of simmering it, completely covered, for three to five hours (for twelve to eighteen pounds, respectively). Plain water is a perfectly fine cooking medium, although Dixie cooks are known to flavor it with

The Loveless Smokehouse

sweet libations from apple cider to Dr. Pepper. (Our personal favorite add-in is a quart or two of Coca-Cola.) Once cooked to the point that a knife slides into it without a lot of force and the bone is slightly loose, the ham should be cooled in its broth for an hour or two. The skin should be cut away along with all but about one-third of an inch of surface fat. (Keep the cut-off fat for making gravy!) It is now ready to slice and eat. (Or, mostly for appearance's sake, it can be glazed with brown sugar and/or molasses and briefly baked.)

In our opinion, the best thing to do with a cooked country ham is to fry some of its cut-off surface fat in a hot iron skillet until mostly rendered then toss in a few quarter-inch-thick slices. When they begin to develop a light, golden crust, remove them and stir a cup of black coffee into the skillet. The resulting red-eye gravy, complete with speckles and bits of ham scraped from the surface of the frying pan, can be poured over the ham slices or served in a bowl alongside the plate for biscuit-dunking or drizzling onto grits.

One final thought about why country ham is so wonderful: although expensive, it is not exclusive. It is a holiday meal and everyday breakfast, equally at home plated on the checkered tablecloths of the Loveless Cafe or on fine linen atop a mahogany dining table. Country ham is true southern soul food that transcends class and status.

AUNT KAT'S SPOON BREAD

Tom says that this variation of spoon is different than many because it calls for scalded milk. "Aunt Kat" is what his nephews call his wife, the "Kat" of TomKat catering.

2	cups milk
1	heaping tablespoon margarine
½	to 1 teaspoon salt
¾	cup cornmeal
4	eggs, separated

Grease a 2-quart baking dish. Scald the milk with the margarine in the top of a double boiler over medium-low heat. Mix the salt and cornmeal with enough water to make a paste in a bowl. Beat the egg yolks in a mixing bowl. Mix in the cornmeal mixture. Add to the milk in the top of the double boiler. Cook until thickened, stirring constantly. Remove the pot from the heat and place it in a pan of cold water. Preheat the oven to 350°F. In a mixing bowl beat the egg whites until stiff. Fold them into the cornmeal mixture. Pour the batter into the prepared baking dish. Place the baking dish in a large skillet of water and bake for 20 to 30 minutes.

MAKES 9 SERVINGS

HEAVENLY CORNBREAD

Cornbread must be made with white cornmeal," Tom says without equivocation. "Yellow cornmeal is Yankee cornmeal. You want to cut the egg into the cornmeal with a fork, and the main thing you are looking for is a batter that is pourable. Mama always says to err on the thin side, to make it like pancake batter. You know, back then when they didn't have anything else, they always had cornbread. Sometimes they would add cracklings to it or whatever else they had on hand. Cornbread became one of your more creative staples. You can do so much with it."

4	*eggs*
3	*cups all-purpose flour*
4	*cups white cornmeal*
1	*cup sugar*
2	*quarts buttermilk*
1½	*tablespoons baking powder*
2	*teaspoons baking soda*
2	*tablespoons salt*
1	*cup canola oil (vegetable oil can be substituted)*
1	*cup shoe peg corn*

Preheat the oven to 375°F. In a mixing bowl beat the eggs with a whisk. Add the flour, cornmeal, sugar, buttermilk, baking powder, baking soda, and salt. Mix thoroughly. Heat the oil and corn until hot. Add to the dry mix. Place in a large, greased pan or two smaller pans and bake for 35 minutes.

MAKES 6 TO 8 SERVINGS

Ed Castleman

Photo Courtesy of Gayle Nash. Used by permission.

We spoke to Ed Castleman late in 2004 about his memories of the home that is now the Loveless Cafe. He didn't recollect much, because he was three years old when his parents moved away. He said he didn't know who built it—"that was a bit before my time"—but he was born there in 1913. At the time his parents were renting the place because his father ran a blacksmith shop and gristmill just across the road. "Not a lot of people remember this, but that area was then called Tank," he said.

Mr. Castleman ate at the Loveless many times over the decades, even into the new century. While he felt the ham wasn't cut as thick as he preferred, he described it as "more than permissible"; and he believed the biscuits, red-eye gravy, and preserves were first rate, as always. When we spoke to him, he mused about the possibility of celebrating his centennial birthday in the Loveless dining room, but in the last week of the year, we received news from Mr. Castleman's family that he had passed away. We are grateful to have had the opportunity to speak to him and get a sense of "Tank" ninety years ago, and we know he'll rest in peace.

Dressings, Relishes, & Preserves

Peach Dressing

Thousand Island Dressing

French Tarragon Dressing

Blue Cheese Dressing

Cranberry-Bourbon Relish

Corn Relish

Sorghum Pepper Relish

Pepper Jelly

Blackberry Preserves

Strawberry Preserves

Peach Preserves

Tartar Sauce

PEACH DRESSING

This recipe is known for its great fresh peach taste.

1	cup frozen peaches	¼	cup honey
2	tablespoons sweet onion	1	cup canola oil
¼	cup cider vinegar		Salt
¼	cup orange juice concentrate		

Place the peaches, onion, vinegar, orange juice, and honey into a food processor. Process the ingredients until smooth and then slowly add the oil while the food processor is running. Add salt to taste.

THOUSAND ISLAND DRESSING

Named for the Thousand Islands of upper New York State, where it originally was invented, this dressing is easy to create from refrigerator-door staples. "If you have ketchup, mayonnaise, relish, and maybe some chopped onions, you've got it made," Tom says. "I've even added ketchup to tartar sauce and pulled it off."

1	cup mayonnaise	1	teaspoon lemon juice
2	tablespoons chili sauce	1	teaspoon Worcestershire sauce
¼	cup sweet relish	2	tablespoons ketchup

Mix the mayonnaise, chili sauce, relish, lemon juice, Worcestershire sauce, and ketchup together until incorporated. Store in a glass container in the refrigerator.

MAKES 2 CUPS

FRENCH TARRAGON DRESSING

Tarragon was always on the shady border of our garden," Tom recalls. "We used in our dressing and also in the baste for lemon-tarragon chicken."

1	tablespoon vinegar	1	teaspoon onion juice
1	tablespoon tarragon vinegar		Capers
	Juice of ½ lemon	½	cup plus 1 tablespoon vegetable oil
1	teaspoon salt		

Combine the vinegar, tarragon vinegar, lemon juice, salt, and onion juice and capers to taste in the work bowl of a food processor. Process until well blended. Add the oil in a fine stream, processing constantly at high speed until completely blended.

MAKES 1 CUP

BLUE CHEESE DRESSING

While different kinds of blue cheese will make a difference in the taste of the dressing, the fact that it is combined with mayonnaise mitigates the power of the cheese. For a more pungent blue cheese flavor in the salad, add a good crumbled cheese atop the dressing.

2	cups mayonnaise	1	teaspoon Worcestershire sauce
2	cups sour cream	1	teaspoon minced garlic
¼	cup buttermilk	¼	teaspoon salt
⅛	cup milk	¼	teaspoon pepper
1	teaspoon lemon juice	¼	pound crumbled blue cheese

In a large bowl combine the mayonnaise, sour cream, buttermilk, milk, lemon juice, Worcestershire sauce, garlic, salt, and pepper. Mix until smooth. Add the blue cheese and mix for 5 minutes.

MAKES 6 TO 8 CUPS

CRANBERRY-BOURBON RELISH

A cranberry salad or relish is almost more important than the turkey in a southern cook's home," Tom advises. "My wife and her grandmother talk more about the importance of the cranberry salad than the turkey itself. Like mashed potatoes, sweet potato casserole, and green beans, it's essential."

2	*pounds whole cranberries, thawed*
8	*oranges, zest removed, and then sliced*
1	*tablespoon ground cinnamon*
2	*to 3 cups sugar*
1	*cup bourbon*

In a 2-inch deep casserole dish, place the cranberries, zests from 2 oranges, slices of the 2 zested oranges, cinnamon, and the sugar. Cover with foil. Bake at 350°F for 1 hour. When the berries are tender, adjust the sugar. Add the bourbon. Cover the pan. Cook for an additional 30 minutes. Squeeze the remaining orange slices into the relish and stir. Remove the zests and seeds.

MAKES 8 SERVINGS

CORN RELISH

Relishes are all about eating from the garden," Tom tells us. "When you are close to the earth and live off what you grow, they are all the more important. They are a way to add flavor and spice to something that is a staple. My kids' great-grandmother puts chow-chow on her field peas."

¼	cup canola oil or ½ stick butter
1	(24-ounce) bag corn (fresh or frozen)
1	onion, diced
1	green bell pepper, diced
1	red bell pepper, diced
1	tablespoon cracked red pepper (hot)
1	tablespoon black pepper
1	tablespoon mustard seed
1	teaspoon celery seed
½	cup sugar
¼	cup apple cider vinegar
¼	cup apple juice or apple cider

Heat the oil or butter in a medium-size pan and sauté the corn, onion, bell peppers, red pepper, black pepper, mustard seed, and celery seed for 5 minutes on medium heat. Add the sugar and let it dissolve, simmering for another 5 minutes. Then add the apple cider vinegar and apple juice, and let the mixture simmer until the liquid is reduced by half.

MAKES 8 TO 12 SERVINGS

SORGHUM PEPPER RELISH

We never had even tasted sorghum until we sat down for breakfast at the Loveless Cafe one morning long ago. There it was on the table, along with honey and the house preserves. It has since become a mainstay in our own cupboard (ordered from *www.LovelessCafe.com*). Tom mused about its importance in southern cooking: "If you look back, there are wives' tales and traditions passed through generations that have to do with sorghum. It used to be a staple through the Civil War and into the Depression, but then it fell out of fashion. Now it's come back as a kind of health food. That is because of the hard-to-find nutrients—B-complex, calcium, iron, and potassium—in sorghum that are found nowhere else. We have customers who request it instead of honey. The belief is that it's less refined than honey, so it has more of the good stuff."

1	*large red bell pepper*
¼	*cup (½ stick) butter*
½	*cup finely chopped onion*
1	*teaspoon cracked red pepper*
2	*tablespoons mustard seed*
1	*tablespoon sorghum syrup*
2	*tablespoons apple cider vinegar*
	Tabasco
	Salt

Roast the pepper over an open flame until the skin blisters and burns. Let the pepper cool until you can rub the skin off. Placing it in a plastic bag first works well. Remove the stem and seeds and chop finely. Heat the butter in a medium saucepan over medium heat and sauté the onions, cracked red pepper, and mustard seed. Add the sorghum and apple cider vinegar and caramelize the mixture. Add the roasted red pepper and the Tabasco and salt to taste and heat through.

MAKES 6 TO 8 SERVINGS

Tom Morales

Photo by Dave Hill. Used by permission.

To regular customers of the Loveless Cafe, to longtime employees, and to hungry travelers in search of a classic Tennessee meal, Tom Morales is a savior.

As we join him at a checkered-cloth-covered table in a dining room filled with customers plowing into plates of fried chicken, country ham, pulled pork, and biscuits, he says with genuine dismay at the very thought: "We might right now be sitting here in a McDonald's or a Hardee's." That was what could have become of the property when the

McCabe family, who had been running the early cafe since 1973, decided that it was time to sell it. Donna McCabe and her son, George, hoped that the place could be taken over by someone who would maintain the tradition that they had inherited from former owners, the Maynard family, who acquired it from founders Lon and Annie Loveless. In fact, at one point before it went on the market, George McCabe had asked Tom Morales if he wanted to buy it and uphold the legacy. At the time, Tom demurred, his hands full running other restaurants as well as the hugely successful movie-production catering company, TomKats.

The Loveless is on a lucrative piece of real estate, and plans were drawn up to transform the property into a strip mall zoned for two fast food outlets. At this news, Tom couldn't help but reconsider. "There is a side of me that's sentimental about history," he says, noting that he grew up nearby and has fond memories of coming to the Loveless with his family in the 1950s. "I felt a community obligation not to let another landmark go. I was compelled to act so we didn't lose this place.

"I had the expertise. A friend had the money. What started as 'Let's-Save-This' turned into a huge responsibility." The money was about three million dollars. In terms of expertise, it is hard to imagine anyone better qualified to do what Tom Morales has done in his resurrection of the beloved restaurant. First, he grew up eating well in a large family of ten children where the men learned to barbecue for two basic reasons: occasionally to relieve mother of the responsibilities of cooking and to get out of her hair in the kitchen. "It was a running joke among my brothers and sisters that as much as we cooked, one of us was going to wind up in the food business. It turned out I was the one."

Prior to the big breakthrough with his catering company, TomKats, Tom and future wife, Kathie, opened their own barbecue restaurant in Prosperity, South Carolina, in 1978. With dry rub inspired by the Rendezvous in Memphis, a low-country mustard-based sauce, a mountain-style tomato-based sauce, and the vinegar-pepper sauce of eastern North Carolina, Uncle Tom's BBQ covered all the barbecue bases. "I really appreciate barbecue," Tom says. "Nobody does it the same, and most of it is at least pretty good." He then went on to run restaurants in Destin, Florida, which put him in eating distance of New Orleans. "We went to Commander's Palace when Paul Prudhomme was there, then to his own K-Paul's," Tom recalls. We saw the beginnings of trends like blackening and the insistence on fresh seafood. I really learned my seafood during five years in Destin, and that has proved to be my edge. I bought boatloads of fish, and I learned that if a boat has been out two weeks, you want the ones on the top."

Tom and Kat moved back to Nashville in 1986, and after a short stint in the world of corporate restaurants, he started a consulting business. He designed a kitchen at Starwood Amphitheater, then took a job running it. "By the end of that summer, I was getting tons of catering calls," he says. "My food was different. People came to events expecting fried catfish or meat with heavy gravy, and I was giving them grilled tuna and other healthy alternatives. At a time when country music videos were coming on the scene, stars were beginning to worry about their waistlines. We catered Dolly Parton's TV series, which gave us a national reference."

Then came a call from a movie production company asking Tom if he had a mobile kitchen, which is of course a requirement for catering on location. He said, sure, he did, then frantically tried to find one. Using a deposit of ten thousand dollars from the movie people, Tom went to Phoenix to pick up a kitchen truck he had bought by reading want ads. "It was a taco wagon!" he exclaims with retrospective humor. "On the side was painted its name: Ricky Ricardo's Chili Express." Tom and his staff painted over the old wording and came up with the TomKats cat logo. They ripped out the old steam tables and set up a double-sided buffet line. "It used to be customary for movie caterers to hand people plates of food, like they were in a prison commissary," he says. "By changing to a help-yourself buffet, out of my own ignorance, I revolutionized the food delivery system on movie sets. We integrated vegetables and earthy-crunchies into the bill of fare. Our reputation spread fast.

"'Help, come down here and feed us!' called a producer from South Carolina one day. 'We are getting nothing but mystery meat and gravy!' All of a sudden, we were doing the biggest movies." Recently, these have included *A Beautiful Mind, Miss Congeniality, Meet the Parents, A League of Their Own,* and the HBO TV series, *Sex and the City.* Earning its early reputation as the healthy caterer, TomKats now dominates the

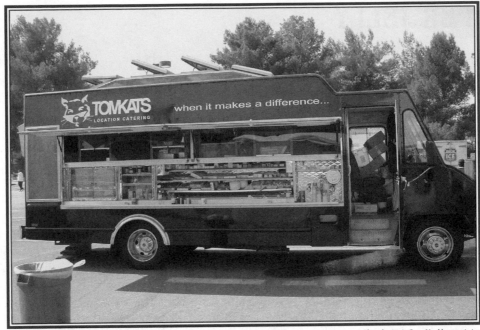

Photo by Angie Gore. Used by permission.

industry. Producers and stars know to count on Tom's company for meals that are a cut above.

The company's vice-president of operations, Jesse Goldstein, believes that work in the business of movie catering is ideal preparation for being part of a well-run restaurant. "The movie drop-outs are the best employees," he explains. "They know the front and back of the house. They know the whole process. They remember that they are there to make people feel well taken care of."

In Tom's words, "You can't hide that you are the maitre d', the chef, dishwasher, server, and on occasion, the mechanic. We are the NFL of foodservice." That conviction makes it easy to believe that the newly born Loveless Cafe is in the best possible hands.

PEPPER JELLY

This combination of hot and sweet works well with cream cheese ... "especially on Ritz crackers," Tom notes.

1	cup chopped green bell peppers		2	(3-ounce) packages liquid fruit pectin
1	cup chopped hot green peppers			Paraffin
7½	cups sugar			
1½	cups (5% acid strength) white vinegar			

Combine the green peppers, hot green peppers, sugar, and vinegar in a Dutch oven. Bring to a boil, reduce the heat to medium low, and cook for 6 minutes, stirring frequently. Stir in the fruit pectin. Cook for 3 minutes longer, stirring frequently. Remove from the heat. Skim off the foam using a metal spoon. Pour the jelly into 6 hot, sterilized half-pint jars, leaving ½ inch headspace. Cover with a ⅛-inch layer of paraffin; seal with 2-piece lids. Heat the jars in a boiling water bath for 10 minutes to seal the lids.

MAKES 6 (½-PINT) JARS

BLACKBERRY PRESERVES

On the subject of berries, Tom Morales has fond memories.

"Collecting blackberries was always a family outing. It was quite a job to protect ourselves from the thorns." He adds, "Berries are a vital part of Southern food lore. Mama Lovorn, my wife's grandmother, who is in her 90s and tells firsthand stories about her grandfather's stories of the Civil War, explained why the sumac berry turns red in the fall. 'Because it has sugar in it,' she said. 'But why does it turn *red*?' we asked. She answered, 'So the birds in the sky can see it.'"

4	cups blackberries (fresh or frozen)
1	cup sugar

Gently rinse the blackberries with cold water. Set in the sink and let dry. Put the berries in a large pot with the sugar. Let sit for 2 hours or until the blackberries release their juices. Bring the blackberries to a simmer on medium heat for 30 to 45 minutes. Gently stir; cook the berries until reduced by half or the mixture reaches jam thickness. Jar the preserves right out of the kettle, filling each jar to the top. Place a top on each jar as tight as possible.

MAKES 4 CUPS

STRAWBERRY PRESERVES

No matter when you come to eat at the Loveless, the table will be set with made-here preserves. "Growing up, I can remember there was a preserve for every growing season," Tom says. "Each berry ripens at a different time, and you preserved the fruit of the day."

4	cups strawberries (fresh or frozen)
1	cup sugar

Gently rinse the strawberries with cold water. Set them in the sink and let dry. Trim the tops off the berries and cut the berries in half. Put the berries in a large pot with the sugar. Let sit for 2 hours or until strawberries release their juices. Bring the strawberries to a simmer on medium heat for 30 to 45 minutes. Gently stir; cook the berries until reduced by half or the mixture reaches jam thickness. Jar the preserves right out of the kettle, filling each jar to the top. Place a top on each jar as tight as possible.

MAKES 4 CUPS

PEACH PRESERVES

Tom jokes, "I believe this is the secret to why the biscuits taste so good at the Loveless: because people put peach preserves on them. This is our signature item."

4	cups canned peaches in syrup
1	pound sugar

Over low heat cook the peaches with syrup, stirring occasionally for 30 to 45 minutes. Do not overstir, or the fruit will break down. Add the sugar and continue to cook over medium heat until reduced by three-quarters or the mixture reaches jam thickness. Jar the preserves right out of the kettle, filling each jar to the top. Place a top on each jar as tight as possible.

MAKES 4 TO 6 CUPS

TARTAR SAUCE

Tartar sauce is taken for granted whenever fried fish is served. Tom puts it bluntly: "Tartar sauce is tartar sauce. It's essential with catfish. It enhances the taste." But then he adds with a wink, "Or . . . can also be used to hide it."

½	cup mayonnaise	Dash of lemon juice
3	tablespoons sweet pickle juice	Dash of Tabasco
2	tablespoons dill pickle relish	Salt and pepper

Combine the mayonnaise, pickle juice, relish, lemon juice and Tabasco, and salt and pepper to taste in a small mixing bowl. Serve in a small condiment bowl or ramekin to accompany your favorite fish.

MAKES 10 SERVINGS

Salads
& Slaws

Ribbon Salad

Fresh Chicken Salad

Cranberry Salad

Cucumbers & Onions

Tomato, Cucumber & Red Onion Salad

Ginger Ale & Grapefruit Salad

Tomato Aspic

Pimiento Cheese

Coleslaw

Sour Slaw

Pool Hall Slaw

Deviled Eggs

Vegetable Chips

Candied Walnuts

RIBBON SALAD

Blue cheese has an assertive flavor that some eaters don't like. But this salad has converted many of them. "It's a ribbon salad, but I call this our BLUE-ribbon salad," Tom says. "The combination of ingredients is refreshing and intriguing, even for those who don't like blue cheese."

1	head iceberg lettuce
1	head romaine lettuce
1	cup Peach Dressing (see page 43)
1	cup Blue Cheese Dressing (see page 44)
½	cup blue cheese crumbles
	Vegetable Chips (see page 74)
1	cup Candied Walnuts (see page 75)

Wash and dry the lettuce. Julienne (or ribbon cut) the lettuce and mix with the peach dressing in a bowl. Then place 4 equal parts on individual chilled plates. Take one-fourth of the blue cheese dressing and drizzle it across each plate in zigzag fashion. Top each plate with 2 tablespoons of the blue cheese crumbles, a few vegetable chips, and one-fourth of the candied walnuts.

MAKES 4 SALADS

FRESH CHICKEN SALAD

The reputation of the Loveless Cafe was to a large extent built on its way with chicken. The preparation most customers know is fried. But cooks in these parts do just about everything with it. "We lived off the yard bird when we were growing up," Tom recalls. "You ate the chicken, and what you didn't eat you made into chicken salad."

4	*(5-ounce) skinless, boneless chicken breasts*	¼	*cup sour cream*
¼	*plus ¼ pound (2 sticks) butter*	3	*tablespoons plus a dash of lemon juice*
	Salt and pepper	¼	*cup cider vinegar*
¼	*cup yellow raisins (optional)*	½	*pound red grapes*
¼	*cup currants (optional)*	½	*pound green grapes*
¼	*cup dried cranberries (optional)*	4	*(12-ounce) bags baby mixed green lettuce*
¼	*cup dried cherries (optional)*	½	*plus ½ cup French Tarragon Dressing (see page 44)*
3	*celery stalks, diced*		
1	*large yellow onion, cut julienne*	2	*large Granny Smith apples, cut into wedges*
2	*teaspoons dried tarragon*		
2	*teaspoons dried oregano*	2	*Red Delicious apples, cut into wedges*
2	*teaspoons dried thyme*		
2	*teaspoons dried basil*	½	*cup candied pecans*
¾	*cup mayonnaise*		

Preheat the oven to 350°F. Place the chicken breasts in a Pyrex baking dish and top them with ¼ pound butter (¼ stick per breast) and salt and pepper to taste. Bake until just done, 20 to 25 minutes. Take the chicken out and let it cool; then dice the meat for salad.

While the chicken is baking, combine the raisins, currants, cranberries, and cherries, if using, and set aside. Sauté the celery, onion, tarragon, oregano, thyme, and basil in the remaining ¼ pound butter on medium heat. Mix the mayonnaise and sour cream together with the 3 tablespoons lemon juice and vinegar. In a large bowl combine the sour cream mixture with the warm sautéed vegetable mixture. Add the chicken and grapes and stir gently. Add the dash of lemon juice and gently stir.

To serve, toss the mixed greens with ½ cup of the vinaigrette dressing and place them on a plate as a base. With a spoon or scoop, portion the chicken salad in the center of the greens on the plate. Drizzle the remaining ½ cup of the vinaigrette on top of the chicken salad. Sprinkle with the dried fruit mixture and garnish with the apple wedges and candied pecans.

MAKES 8 SERVINGS

CRANBERRY SALAD

Y ou have violated a southern tradition if this is not served with your turkey," Tom declares.

1	orange
2	cups cranberries
1½	cups sugar
1	(3-ounce) package lemon gelatin

Peel the orange; remove the seeds. Process the orange and the cranberries in a food processor until finely chopped. Add the sugar and mix well. Let stand for 1 hour. Dissolve the gelatin in 2 cups warm water in a small bowl. Stir into the cranberry mixture. Pour into a nonstick mold. Chill, covered, until set. Unmold onto a serving plate.

MAKES 8 SERVINGS

Variation: You may add chopped pecans if you desire.

CUCUMBERS & ONIONS

The summer garden's yield is at the heart of this refreshing salad, especially welcome on a hot day. Tom: "We can live off garden cucumbers through most of the summer. A dish of cucumbers and onions can take the place of a salad."

3	large cucumbers
1	small or ½ large yellow onion
1	cup apple cider vinegar
½	cup sugar
½	teaspoon salt
1	teaspoon pepper
	Dash of fresh lemon juice

Cut the cucumbers into ½-inch rounds. You may use a peeler and alternate strips for decoration. Cut the onion into thin slices of half-rings. Heat the vinegar and sugar to melt the sugar. (Do not boil.) When cooled, toss the mixture over the cucumbers and onions, stirring gently to combine. Add the salt and pepper and the dash of fresh lemon juice at the end. Serve chilled.

MAKES 8 TO 10 SERVINGS

TOMATO, CUCUMBER & RED ONION SALAD

Here is an early summer salad that takes advantage of a garden's fresh yield.

1	red onion, cut in ¼-inch wedges
4	cucumbers, peeled and sliced in ½-inch rounds
3	Roma tomatoes, cored and cut in ½-inch wedges
½	teaspoon kosher salt
½	teaspoon black pepper
¾	cup cider vinegar
6	tablespoons sugar
2	tablespoons canola oil
1	tablespoon chopped parsley

Soak the red onion wedges in salted ice water for 30 minutes and then drain well. Put the onion, cucumbers, and tomatoes in a large bowl and season with the salt and pepper. Mix together the vinegar, sugar, and canola oil in a small bowl until the sugar is dissolved. Add to the vegetables and toss well. Refrigerate. To serve, add the chopped parsley and toss.

MAKES 5 TO 6 SERVINGS

GINGER ALE & GRAPEFRUIT SALAD

A hot summer's day salad that is great served with grilled chicken breasts, or topped with shrimp.

2	tablespoons unflavored gelatin
¼	cup cold water
½	cup boiling water
¼	cup sugar
¼	cup lemon juice
1	cup ginger ale
1	(20-ounce) can grapefruit sections
8	maraschino cherries

Soften the gelatin in the cold water in a bowl. Add the boiling water, stirring until the gelatin dissolves. Add the sugar and lemon juice; mix well. Stir in the ginger ale. Add the undrained grapefruit. Pour into a serving bowl. Chill, covered, until set. Arrange the maraschino cherries decoratively over the top before serving.

MAKES 8 SERVINGS

Grand Ole Opry

Look at the walls in the foyer of the Loveless Cafe and you see stars. Pictures of celebrities who have eaten there and love it are everywhere. Many of the faces got famous as members of the Grand Ole Opry, Nashville's best-known contribution to American popular culture. More than a music venue, the Opry has helped define "country" as a lifestyle that includes everything from boots and jeans to biscuits and gravy. People who journey from all over America (and the world) to bask in country values come with the joy and purpose of pilgrims because the Grand Ole Opry feels like a spiritual home.

The Opry was named in the fall of 1927, when WSM radio broadcast an hour of classical music hosted by New York Philharmonic conductor Walter Damrosch. Dr. Damrosch apologized to listeners for one of the compositions they heard, a modernistic piece that attempted to be the musical equivalent of a speeding locomotive. "There is no room for realism in serious music," the conductor declared. The next show scheduled to go on the air, broadcast live from studio A in Nashville, began with a steamboat whistle and harmonica blues by DeFord Bailey (who could perfectly evoke a locomotive with his mouth harp), then went on to feature three hours of guitar pickin', minstrel comedians, fiddlers, foot stompers, and backwoods yodelers. The announcer, George D. Hay, began the program by responding to Dr. Damrosch: "From here on out for the next three hours we will present nothing but realism. It will be down to earth for the earthy." He said, "For the past hour we have been listening to music taken largely from Grand Opera, but from now on we will present the Grand Ole Opry."

The Grand Ole Opry, as the show was called from that moment on, was not the first barn dance radio show on the air, but by the 1930s, when the WSM signal had grown from one thousand to fifty thousand watts, it had become the flagship of the country sound. Most of the early acts were instrumentalists with fiddles, banjos, and guitars—groups with such names as the Fruit Jar Drinkers, the Possum Hunters, and the Dixie Clodhoppers. When Roy Acuff joined the Opry troupe in 1938 (performers auditioned to become members of the Opry), the spotlight of the show shifted to vocalists and from string-band music (which always remained part of the repertoire) to the style of white man's blues that was then known vaguely as folk music and only later got named "country."

Some of the Opry's biggest names are Ernest Tubb, Loretta Lynn, Dolly Parton, Marty Robbins, Hank Snow, Charley Pride, Johnny Cash, and, of course, Hank Williams. Comedians have always been a staple of the show, too, from Jam Up and Honey (minstrels in the early days) to country doyenne Minnie Pearl and the Duke of Paducah (Whitey Ford).

Aside from its stable of performers, one thing that makes the Grand Ole Opry unique is that it has always been a real place. Those who listened to it on the radio with religious devotion every weekend knew they could make the journey to Nashville and actually be there, side by side with other country fans and close to the performers whom they loved. When it first went on the air, it was conceived strictly as a radio show and only a handful of local curiosity-seekers came to see it broadcast live. But as the program grew more popular on the airwaves, visiting it in person became a ritual. In 1943, the year Grand Ole Opry broadcasts first went national, *Newsweek* reported: "Uncle Jimmy has since died, but every Saturday night for seventeen years mountaineers and their wives and children have streamed down from the hills on foot, wagon, or jalopy to Nashville to listen to the folk-music festival."

In the early 1930s, the show had moved from a broadcast studio in Nashville to the Hillsboro Theater, then to a series of music halls, and finally, in 1943, to Nashville's downtown Ryman Auditorium. It was at the Ryman that the Grand Ole Opry became an American institution. Built by Captain Thomas G. Ryman in 1892 as a venue for an evangelist named Sam Jones, and originally known as the Union Gospel Tabernacle, the Ryman was a big hall with wooden bench seats and an "1897 Confederate Gallery" balcony that had been installed to accommodate a huge Confederate veterans' reunion. Shows were put on twice a week, and as much as fans loved the place, it was a brutal venue for performers and listeners alike. In the summer, temperatures inside surpassed 120 degrees; teams of nurses were kept on duty to revive people who passed out; included among the backstage crew were employees whose only job was to mop the faces of performers.

The Ryman Auditorium in 1973. Photo by Les Leverett and courtesy of the Grand Ole Opry Archives. Used by permission.

By the late 1960s, executives at WSM were getting worried that the old hall might simply fall apart one weekend. Program director Elmer Alley, who was in charge of broadcasts from the Opry, hated the rickety place because it was a technical nightmare, unsuited for television broadcasts. At the time, the Opry was merely a four-times-a-week event, but Alley thought it could be made into more. He and WSM president Irving Waugh conceived not just a new, modern auditorium, but a whole Grand Ole Opry environment. "Put it on a piece of property that somehow typifies the Tennessee countryside," Alley suggested. "Make it part of a theme park. Have it offer live entertainment, with all kinds of music and dancing."

And so Opryland was born. In 1974 the Grand Ole Opry moved to a new, acoustically sophisticated auditorium far from Ryman and downtown Nashville where it became the centerpiece of a four-hundred-acre theme park and a magnet that still helps fill the Opryland Hotel, the largest nongaming hotel in the world. The Ryman itself, shuttered for two decades, was refurbished in 1994 and reborn as "The Mother Church of Country Music," once again host to country and gospel, as well as pop, jazz, and soul.

Del McCoury onstage at the Grand Ole Opry in 2002. Photo by Chris Hollo and courtesy of the Grand Ole Opry Archives. Used by permission.

TOMATO ASPIC

When tomatoes start to ripen, you have so many that you need to know six different things to do with them," Tom says, describing this aspic as a great summer dish.

8	ripe tomatoes, chopped
1	yellow onion, diced
1	cup diced celery
1	garlic clove, chopped
3	bay leaves
5	whole black peppercorns
5	whole cloves
1	tablespoon kosher salt
3	cups plus ¼ cup tomato juice
1	tablespoon sugar
1	tablespoon cider vinegar
1	tablespoon lemon juice
2	tablespoons unflavored gelatin

Put the tomatoes, onion, celery, garlic, bay leaves, peppercorns, cloves, salt, and 3 cups tomato juice together in a saucepan and bring to a simmer over medium heat for 20 to 30 minutes. Strain the simmered tomato stock through a fine-mesh strainer. This makes about 4½ cups. Add the sugar, vinegar, and lemon juice to the tomato stock and simmer for 10 minutes. Mix the gelatin with the remaining ¼ cup tomato juice until softened. Add the softened gelatin to the simmering stock. Stir 2 to 3 minutes to dissolve the gelatin. Remove from the heat and place in a bowl of ice water to cool. Chill until it begins to thicken. Stir together to mix all ingredients evenly. Pour the aspic into a large Jell-O ring mold or six small Jell-O molds and refrigerate overnight.

MAKES 5 CUPS (10 [½-CUP] MOLDS)

PIMIENTO CHEESE

Any true southern mother of the Loveless generation has her own recipe for pimiento cheese," Tom declares. "It's something like 'pool hall slaw'—a sour slaw made with mustard and vinegar—in that it is something people made because it lasted. Before processed cheese, it was a chore to make your own pimiento cheese. Processed American cheese made it easier to mix, but I believe that making it is becoming a lost art. People ask me, 'Why make it?' My answer is that it *should be made*. It is a tradition. When I fix a grilled cheese sandwich, it wouldn't be right without pimiento cheese."

½   cup grated yellow Cheddar cheese

2½   cups grated extra-sharp white Cheddar cheese

⅛   teaspoon cayenne

¾   cup mayonnaise

3   tablespoons crushed dried pimiento

       Salt and pepper

Stir together the cheeses, cayenne, mayonnaise, pimiento, and salt and pepper to taste in a mixing bowl. Mix well until creamy. Serve chilled; great on white toast.

MAKES 4 TO 6 SERVINGS

COLESLAW

Coleslaw is a major issue throughout the nation, but especially in the South, where the variations are nearly as diverse as different kinds of barbecue. "The entrée and your own taste determine which slaw is best," Tom says. "This one is good with barbecue, on the side or in a sandwich along with the pork."

¼	cup apple cider vinegar
¼	cup sugar
½	cup mayonnaise
½	cup fresh lemon juice
2	teaspoons celery seed
2	tablespoons chopped parsley
½	head green cabbage, shredded and chopped
2	carrots, grated
	Salt and pepper

Pour the vinegar into a saucepan over medium heat. Add the sugar and stir until dissolved. Pour the vinegar mixture into a mixing bowl. Add the mayonnaise, lemon juice, celery seed, and parsley. Stir to combine. Fold in the cabbage and carrots. Add the salt and pepper to taste. Serve chilled.

MAKES 6 TO 8 SERVINGS

SOUR SLAW

On my barbecue sandwich, I like a sour slaw," Tom reveals about this recipe. "Different slaws for different people."

¼	cup vegetable oil
¼	cup white wine vinegar
1	tablespoon dry sherry
2	teaspoons water
2	garlic cloves, peeled and finely chopped
1	tablespoon sugar
1	teaspoon salt
½	head green cabbage, cored and thinly sliced (about 8 cups)
¼	cup chopped parsley

Put oil, vinegar, sherry, water, garlic, sugar, and salt into a blender and purée until smooth. Put the cabbage in large bowl and sprinkle the parsley on top. Pour the dressing over the slaw and toss well. Refrigerate for at least 1 hour before serving.

MAKES 6 TO 8 SERVINGS

POOL HALL SLAW

Tom attributes this recipe to a little dive in west Tennessee that was known for its hamburgers. They were served in the same way barbecue sandwiches are served in that region, topped with cole slaw rather than with lettuce and tomato.

1	*large onion thinly sliced*
¼	*cup apple cider vinegar*
¼	*cup white vinegar*
2	*tablespoons sugar*
1	*tablespoon salt*
2	*tablespoons prepared mustard*
2	*tablespoons mayonnaise*
1	*head green cabbage cored and thinly sliced*

Place the onion, vinegar, sugar, and salt in a saucepan over medium-high heat. Cook until the onion is tender and the liquid is reduced by half (approximately 5 minutes total cooking time). Set aside and let it steep for a few minutes. Add the mustard and stir. Let it cool a few minutes longer and add the mayonnaise and stir. Take the mixture and fold in with the cabbage. Place in the refrigerator until ready to serve or at least 30 minutes. The slaw should have a mustard color and is great on a pulled pork sandwich or a hamburger.

MAKES 8 TO 10 SERVINGS

DEVILED EGGS

Never underestimate the term *deviled*. To a cook it means highly seasoned or taking something healthful and good and "deviling" it with wanton ingredients. Most cooks know deviled eggs, but none take them as seriously as do cooks in the South. "There has always been a competition about who makes the best," Tom observes. "They are like apple pie: Every cook has a favorite special recipe."

6	eggs
¼	cup mayonnaise
3	tablespoons yellow mustard
1	tablespoon sweet pickle relish or dill pickle relish
1	teaspoon cider vinegar
2	teaspoons finely diced yellow onion
	Cayenne
	Salt and pepper
1	teaspoon paprika

Hard-boil the eggs for approximately 7 minutes. Place them under cool running water and tap the eggs to peel them while they are still warm. After peeling the eggs, cut them in half lengthwise, placing the yolks in a separate bowl. Be careful to keep the egg whites in good shape for stuffing. You may want to cook a couple of extra eggs for stuffing later just in case you tear one of your egg whites. Place the egg yolks, mayonnaise, mustard, pickle relish, apple cider vinegar, onion, and cayenne, and salt and pepper to taste in a bowl. Mix well. Spoon the yolk mixture into the egg-white halves neatly, filling the inside. Sprinkle the top with the paprika for color.

MAKES 12 EGG HALVES

VEGETABLE CHIPS

Vegetable chips make a salad more colorful. They were originally part of the TomKats catering menu, but are perfectly appropriate at the Loveless Cafe, where the fundamental belief is to remain true to local ingredients and produce from local gardens.

1	carrot
1	potato
	Peanut oil
	Salt

Peel the carrot and potato. Then use the carrot peeler to shave the ingredients into thin, lengthwise chips. Pour enough peanut oil to cover a skillet 1-inch deep. Heat the oil to 350°F and deep-fry the chips until just about golden brown, just like potato chips. Salt the chips when taking them out of the grease. Drain on paper towels. These chips can be made ahead of time and stored in a sealed container.

MAKES 4 TO 6 SERVINGS

CANDIED WALNUTS

Walnuts store well and are available to cooks year-round. Like pecans, they are a cook's staple.

1	cup walnuts
½	cup confectioners' sugar plus more for blanching
1	teaspoon cayenne plus more for blanching
1	tablespoon salt
	Peanut oil

Blanch the walnuts by putting them in a heavy saucepan. Add some confectioners' sugar and cayenne to taste. Cover with water. Bring to a boil and then simmer for 15 minutes. Drain in a colander. Heat 1 inch of the peanut oil in a skillet to 350°F. Mix ½ cup confectioners' sugar, the 1 teaspoon cayenne, and the salt in a stainless steel mixing bowl. Add the blanched walnuts and toss until evenly coated. Fry the nuts immediately in the oil for 8 to 10 minutes.

MAKES 4 TO 6 SERVINGS

Note: The same oil used for the vegetable chips can be reused.

Mary Elizabeth Roberts

Mary holding her great grand-mother's sorghum bottle.

With five daughters, four sons, and twenty-six grandchildren, you'd think that Mary Elizabeth Roberts would have her hands too full to pay attention to work at the Loveless Cafe. But there isn't a long-standing employee in the house who is more a part of the operation than this blue-eyed charmer who has kept in touch with everything that goes on in front and in the kitchen. In fact, you might say that being part of the Loveless is a family tradition. Mary's daughter worked here. Her granddaughter Cissy works here. And one of Cissy's daughters works here, too. The other daughter isn't old enough yet!

Mary's memories of the Loveless go back decades. Long ago, it was her job to open up before dawn and turn on the stove. She's made the biscuits but says that her main claim to fame in the kitchen was her way with ham and eggs and grits. "I've always loved the work," she declares. "Somehow I never had the will to stay at home."

Mary was away from the business for several years before the renovation, but when it was ready to reopen, she came back. With new owner Tom Morales looking for ways to make a strong and meaningful connection with the best of the restaurant's past, Mary Elizabeth's presence was a precious gift. "I come in every day but Sunday," she says. "I work anywhere they need me." And sure enough, during a week we spent at the tables and in the kitchen and prep areas of the Loveless Cafe, Mary was ubiquitous. She chats with old friends who come in to eat, offers encouragement and advice to the staff, clears a table when a table needs clearing, and immeasurably adds to the caring spirit of this kindly restaurant.

Gravies, Sauces & Rubs

Vinegar Hot Sauce

Loveless Barbecue Sauce

Low-Country Barbecue Sauce

Red-Eye Gravy

Sausage Gravy

Chicken Gravy

Pan Milk Gravy

Turkey Gravy

Backstrap Molasses Glaze

Wet Brine

Loveless Seasoned Salt

Loveless Dry Rub

VINEGAR HOT SAUCE (FOR PULLED PORK)

How to sauce—or not to sauce—barbecue is a topic about which every pit master has strong opinions. Having grown up in Nashville, run a barbecue restaurant in South Carolina, and traveled all over the U.S. sampling the regional varieties, Tom Morales is an expert.

"Vinegar pepper hot sauce is a tradition in eastern North Carolina," he explains. "I start out all pulled pork with it because it keeps the meat moist. If you want, you can even put a tomato-based, red sauce on top of it. This is a balanced recipe, and the apple cider vinegar is the key. Use too much and it will taste too vinegary, but not enough will defeat the purpose. The sauce needs bite, because it is pork's exclamation point."

1	cup water
2	tablespoons salt
½	cup apple cider vinegar
½	tablespoon Louisiana hot sauce
1	tablespoon black pepper
1	tablespoon chopped fresh oregano
¼	cup firmly packed light brown sugar
1	tablespoon Loveless Dry Rub (see page 88)
1	tablespoon granulated garlic

Bring the water, salt, vinegar, hot sauce, pepper, oregano, brown sugar, dry rub, and garlic to a boil and stop the cooking. Serve with pulled pork (see page 108).

MAKES ABOUT 1½ CUPS (ENOUGH FOR 8 TO 10 POUNDS OF PORK)

LOVELESS BARBECUE SAUCE

Tom likes this recipe because it is flexible. "It's an all-purpose barbecue sauce," he says. "You can make a condensed, hot version for pork by doubling up on the peppers. Otherwise, in its milder form, you might use it on chicken. For the mustard-based sauce of central South Carolina, we simply reverse the amounts of mustard and ketchup."

2	*cups diced yellow onions*
¼	*cup diced green bell peppers*
¼	*cup diced red bell peppers*
½	*to 1 teaspoon crushed dried red pepper*
2	*tablespoons canola oil or ¼ pound (1 stick) butter*
1	*tablespoon chopped garlic*
½	*to 1 teaspoon chili powder*
¼	*cup black pepper*
½	*cup firmly packed light brown sugar*
½	*cup firmly packed dark brown sugar*
1	*cup honey*
¼	*cup molasses*
½	*cup apple cider vinegar*
1	*cup salt water (⅓ cup salt to 1 cup water)*
1	*tablespoon yellow mustard*
	Juice of 1 lemon
1	*tablespoon Worcestershire sauce*
6	*cups ketchup*

Sauté the onions, peppers, and crushed red pepper in the canola oil over medium heat until lightly browned, 5 to 10 minutes. Add the garlic and simmer for 5 minutes more. Add the chili powder, black pepper, brown sugars, honey, and molasses and cook until caramelized. Add the vinegar, salt water, mustard, lemon juice, and Worcestershire and simmer for 15 minutes. Add the ketchup and simmer for 10 minutes. Let cool.

MAKES 8 TO 10 CUPS

LOW-COUNTRY BARBECUE SAUCE

Mustard-based sauce is a South Carolina specialty, popular in the Low Country and up to around Columbia. North and west of that, tomato-based is more common. Tom comments that sauce is important, but "I always have felt like the true test of good barbecue is that the meat stands alone."

2	*tablespoons minced garlic*
¾	*cup chopped green bell pepper*
1½	*cups finely diced Vidalia onions*
2	*tablespoons vegetable oil*
1	*tablespoon crushed red pepper*
½	*cup dark brown sugar*
½	*cup light brown sugar*
2	*tablespoons honey*
2	*tablespoons molasses*
½	*cup apple cider vinegar*
4	*cups prepared mustard*
½	*cup ketchup*
1	*tablespoon Worcestershire sauce*
½	*cup water*
2	*tablespoons salt*
1	*tablespoon black pepper*

Sweat the garlic, green bell pepper, and onions in the vegetable oil over medium heat. Add the crushed red pepper. Add the brown sugars, honey, and molasses and caramelize the mixture. Add the vinegar and let simmer for about 15 minutes. Add the mustard, ketchup, Worcestershire sauce, water, salt, and black pepper and simmer until reduced by one-fourth.

MAKES 8 SERVINGS

RED-EYE GRAVY

Tom explains that the gravy got its name because when you cook a slice of ham in a pan, the ham bone, surrounded by the ham's juices, looks like a red eye. Red eye gravy is known for its thin consistency.

1	tablespoon vegetable oil
1	(¼ inch thick) bone-in center cut country ham slice
½	cup brewed coffee
1	cup water
2	to 3 teaspoons brown sugar

Place the oil in a skillet over medium-high heat. Add the ham slice and cook for 3 to 4 minutes on both sides until ham is browned. Remove the ham from the skillet. To the drippings in the skillet, add the brewed coffee, water, and brown sugar. Bring to a boil and cook until the sugar dissolves. Serve with country ham, biscuits, eggs any style and stone ground grits.

MAKES 4 TO 6 SERVINGS

SAUSAGE GRAVY

This gravy is great with biscuits, grits, and mashed potatoes.

½	pound pork sausage		Salt
2	tablespoons all-purpose flour	½	tablespoon black pepper
1	cup milk	1	teaspoon cayenne

In a skillet over medium heat, cook the pork sausage and crumble into small pieces. Add the flour and cook for 5 minutes. Add the milk and bring to a simmer. Add salt to taste, black pepper, and cayenne and stir until blended.

MAKES 4 SERVINGS

The motel is history, but this great old sign on Highway 100 remains a beacon of hospitality. Hot biscuits and country ham are forever!

Built as a private home a century ago, subsequently known as the Harpeth Valley Tea Room, the Loveless Cafe found its culinary destiny in the mid-twentieth century when Lon and Annie Loveless started serving fried chicken to travelers passing by.

Gerri Meisel is at the counter ready to greet customers at the front door. To her right and left are signed photographs by some of the Loveless Cafe's many celebrity fans.

"Hams & Jams" is adjacent to the cafe and offers visitors an opportunity to shop for groceries to make country-style meals at home or to buy ready-to-eat meals for picnics. Loveless products are also available by mail order (800-889-2432) and at www.lovelesscafe.com.

A few breakfast choices, from the top:
a waffle, an omelet (see page 22),
and a plate of country ham (page 107)

Carol Fay Ellison brushes butter atop biscuits before they go in the oven.

In middle Tennessee, fried chicken (see page 118) is popular for breakfast as well as for lunch, supper, picnics, tailgate parties, and midnight snacks.

Ribbon Salad (see page 57)

Fried Green Tomato BLT (see page 120)

True Southern Vegetables, clockwise from upper left: black-eye peas (see page 155), skillet-fried shoepeg corn, caramel sweet potatoes (see page 139), greens with pot liquor (see page 146)

Shrimp and grits

Pork butts basking in hickory smoke

A pulled pork platter (see page 108)

Banana pudding
with house-made wafers
(see page 182)

Coconut pie:
de rigueur after a
smokehouse meal
(see page 173)

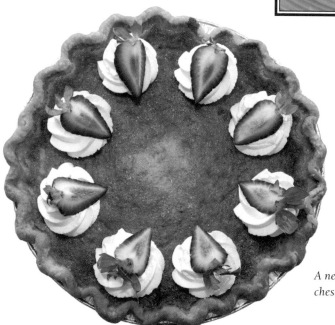

A necessary Southern dessert:
chess pie (see page 191)

CHICKEN GRAVY

When cooking Loveless Fried Chicken, all the debris that remains in the bottom of the skillet once the meat is removed is essential for making pan gravy. This gravy is great on mashed potatoes, rice, and, of course, fried chicken.

2	*tablespoons butter*
2	*tablespoons all-purpose flour*
6	*cups chicken stock*
1	*tablespoon black pepper*
	Salt

Make a light roux by heating the butter over medium heat and adding the flour. Cook until beige in color. After frying some chicken add the chicken stock to the pan with fried chicken drippings. Bring to simmer and add the black pepper, salt to taste, and light roux. Cook the gravy for 5 to 10 minutes, whipping until smooth. This gravy goes well with Fried Chicken (page 118).

MAKES 6 CUPS

PAN MILK GRAVY

There is no substitute for making gravy from the drippings in a cast iron skillet, whether you've cooked fried chicken or country-fried steak. Pan gravy is rich, peppery, and a wonderful dip for biscuits, too.

½   *cup reserved beef pan drippings and oil*

¼   *cup all-purpose flour*

1   *cup whole milk plus more for thickening*

1   *teaspoon salt*

½   *teaspoon black pepper*

After cooking country-fried steak (see page 121), pour (or leave) ½ cup pan drippings and oil in the skillet over medium heat. Add the flour and stir until well mixed and pasty. Add the whole milk, salt, and pepper and bring to a slow boil. Add more milk until you have the desired consistency; we prefer a thicker gravy. Pour the gravy over your meat and/or potatoes while hot. It goes well with Country-Fried Steak.

MAKES ABOUT 2 CUPS

TURKEY GRAVY

Turkey without gravy would be as wrong as ham without biscuits. Gravy is essential for ladling on the meat, the dressing, and the mashed potatoes, and is also the key ingredient in leftover hot turkey sandwiches.

	Giblets from one turkey
4	*cups water*
2	*celery stalks, whole*
2	*carrot sticks, whole*
1	*large yellow onion, quartered*
2	*tablespoons salt*
1	*teaspoon black pepper*
½	*teaspoon white pepper*
1	*whole garlic clove , peeled*
1	*cup canola oil*
½	*cup all-purpose flour*

Place the giblets in a saucepan and cover with water. Bring to a boil and add the celery, carrots, onion, salt, black and white pepper, and garlic. Reduce the heat and cook for 30 minutes at a slow boil adding water if necessary. Strain the ingredients, reserving the stock. Heat the oil in a skillet over medium heat. Add the flour and stir until well mixed. Stir in 2 cups of the reserved stock and continue stirring at a slow boil until the gravy thickens. Add more stock until desired consistency is reached; we prefer a less thick but not soupy gravy for our turkey. Serve with Turkey & Carol Fay's Biscuit and Cornbread Stuffing on page 126.

MAKES ABOUT 4 CUPS

Variation: For a good lunch dish add leftover turkey meat to the gravy and serve over white bread.

BLACKSTRAP MOLASSES GLAZE

Molasses is used in Loveless barbecue sauce and is an essential ingredient of the kitchen's glaze.

"We use blackstrap molasses glaze on whole grilled chickens and chicken breasts," Tom says. "It's a variation of barbecue sauce, but it packs a strong sweetness because of the intensity of the molasses. We use a 5-ounce chicken breast. We grill it with the skin on because it stays moist. We add the glaze."

3	*cups apple cider*
½	*cup dark molasses*
¼	*cup cider vinegar*
1	*cup barbecue sauce*

To make the glaze, bring the apple cider to a boil and reduce the heat to a medium simmer, cooking until syrupy and reduced to about ½ cup. Add the molasses, vinegar, and barbecue sauce. Simmer 10 minutes.

MAKES 4 TO 6 CUPS

WET BRINE

We brine our chicken because it helps condition the meat," Tom advises. "A short brine doesn't impart flavor; it is more for cleaning the meat. It draws out the blood. An overnight brine will impart flavor."

1	gallon water
½	cup apple cider vinegar
1	cup kosher salt
½	cup sugar
10	cloves
1	tablespoon crushed juniper berries
6	fresh sprigs thyme
6	bay leaves
2	tablespoons crushed dried red pepper
½	cup chopped fresh parsley
1	tablespoon whole allspice
2	tablespoons black pepper

Heat the water. Add the salt, sugar, vinegar, cloves, juniper berries, thyme, bay leaves, red pepper, parsley, allspice, and pepper. Stir until the salt and sugar are dissolved. Marinate the pork loin (see page 114) for at least 1 hour before you drain and cook.

MAKES 1½ GALLONS

LOVELESS SEASONED SALT

Tom cautions to use this salt judiciously. "Remember: You can't take salt out, but you can always add it." It can be purchased at *www.lovelesscafe.com*.

1	cup kosher salt	½	tablespoon rubbed sage
⅓	cup garlic salt	1	teaspoon dried rosemary
3	tablespoons celery salt	1½	tablespoons dried oregano
2	tablespoons dry mustard	1	teaspoon dried thyme

Blend together the kosher salt, garlic salt, celery salt, dry mustard, sage, rosemary, oregano, and thyme. Store in air-tight container.

MAKES 1¼ CUPS

LOVELESS DRY RUB

This rub is for pork butt, pork loins, ribs, and turkey breasts. It can be purchased at *www.LovelessCafe.com*.

1	(12-ounce) box light brown sugar	2	cups Loveless Seasoned Salt
1½	cups granulated garlic	1	cup chili powder
1	cup black pepper	¼	cup celery salt
1	cup thyme	¼	cup fennel seed
2	cups chopped fresh oregano	¼	cup paprika

Mix together the brown sugar, garlic, pepper, thyme, oregano, seasoned salt, chili powder, celery salt, salt, fennel seed, and paprika. Store in an airtight container until ready to use. When ready, rub the seasoning into both sides of your meat and then rub any residue and additional mix until your meat is covered. It is then ready to cook.

MAKES 10 CUPS

Soups

Split Pea Soup & Country Ham

Tomato-Basil Soup

Traditional Tomato Soup

Black-Eyed Pea & Country Ham Chowder

Chicken Stock

Potato-Leek Soup

Oyster Stew

Chicken & Dumplings

Roasted Butternut Squash Soup with Cornbread Croutons

Crawfish Bisque

SPLIT PEA SOUP & COUNTRY HAM

Although the southern growing season lasts most of the year, there are months when nothing much is coming up from the garden. "Here is a soup you can make in the dead of winter," Tom suggests. "You've dried your peas and beans, and your country ham was preserved and smoked. It's all from the larder."

2	to 2½ pounds country ham (bone in)
4	bay leaves
1	pound split peas, picked over and rinsed
3	red potatoes, diced into ½-inch cubes
1	teaspoon dried thyme
2	tablespoons olive oil
2	cups medium-diced onions
2	medium carrots, diced
2	teaspoons chopped garlic
2	celery stalks, medium diced
1	tablespoon butter
2	teaspoons sugar
	Salt and black pepper
	Balsamic vinegar

In a large stockpot, combine the ham, bay leaves, and 3 quarts of water. Bring to a boil. Reduce the heat to a low simmer until the meat is tender (about 2½ hours). Remove the ham from the stock and pick it into bite-size pieces. Add the split peas, potatoes, and thyme to the stock. Cook until tender, about 20 minutes. In a large sauté pan heat the olive oil on medium high. Sauté the onions, carrots, garlic, and celery. Add the butter and sugar. Cook the vegetables until caramelized, 12 to 15 minutes. Add the vegetables and potatoes to the split-pea pot. Simmer until the potatoes are tender, about 10 minutes. Add the salt and pepper to taste and a splash of balsamic vinegar.

MAKES 6 TO 8 SERVINGS

TOMATO-BASIL SOUP

Tom feels slightly disloyal discussing this variation of tomato soup because it contains no potatoes. "Traditionalists argue that you must have potatoes and sautéed onions in tomato soup. That is how it always begins. But this recipe is a New-South take on the old way of doing it."

2	yellow onions, finely diced
5	tablespoons unsalted butter
2	teaspoons salt
½	teaspoon black pepper
3	tablespoons plus a dash of sugar
1	(15-ounce) can crushed tomatoes
4	cups water
1	cup heavy cream
4	basil leaves, cut julienne

In a large saucepan over medium heat, sauté the onions in butter until clear and softened. Add the salt, pepper, and 3 tablespoons of the sugar. Cook until the sugar is dissolved, about 5 minutes. After 2 minutes, add the tomatoes and a dash of sugar and cook for 5 minutes. Add the water. Simmer for 15 minutes. Set the soup aside to cool. When cooled, purée the soup in a blender. Return the soup to the stove, simmer 5 minutes, and then add the cream. Sprinkle the basil for garnish.

MAKES 4 TO 6 SERVINGS

TRADITIONAL TOMATO SOUP

For traditional tomato soup, potatoes and onions are as essential as stewed tomatoes. Canned tomatoes can be used, but the origins of this recipe go back to the dilemma faced by cooks whose gardens bore so many tomatoes that they were pressed to find varied ways to use them.

2	tablespoons butter
1	onion, chopped
1	large Idaho potato, diced
1	cup chicken stock or water
1	(14½-ounce) can stewed tomatoes
1	(14½-ounce) can tomatoes
	Dash of sugar
	Salt and pepper

In a stockpot place the butter, onion, and potato over medium heat. Stir until the onion is translucent. Add the chicken stock and bring to a medium boil. Place the tomatoes in a blender and pulse to remove any chunks. Add the tomatoes with their juice and sugar to the stockpot. Add salt and pepper to taste. Return to a boil and then reduce the heat to simmer for 15 to 20 minutes. The thickness can be adjusted by adding water, chicken stock, or tomato juice. Serve with cornbread patties.

MAKES 4 TO 6 SERVINGS

BLACK-EYED PEA & COUNTRY HAM CHOWDER

Typically, black-eyed peas are abundant in the cupboard and a country ham is in short supply. This recipe is a way to use plenty of the former and a measured amount of the latter.

2	tablespoons butter
1½	cups diced onions
1	garlic clove, diced
1½	tablespoons chopped jalapeño peppers
1	cup diced celery
1	cup diced carrot
1	cup chopped country ham
4	cups chicken stock
1	tablespoon dried thyme
¾	teaspoon celery seed
½	teaspoon black pepper
1	bay leaf
1½	pounds black-eyed peas
2	cups diced potatoes
1	cup half-and-half

Melt the butter in a large pot over medium heat. Add the onions, garlic, and jalapeños. Cook for 5 minutes. Add the celery, carrots, and ham. Stir in the chicken stock, thyme, celery seed, black pepper, bay leaf, and black-eyed peas. Bring to a boil. Reduce to simmer, and cook 20 minutes. Add the potatoes. Simmer for 25 minutes and then add the half-and-half. If more liquid is needed, add more cream or water.

MAKES 6 TO 8 SERVINGS

CHICKEN STOCK

Chicken stock is the basis of just about everything," Tom advises. "You're living off the land, on the farm. What you have is what you are and it is what you eat. Chicken stock is an example of using everything. You boil the chicken, and so you have chicken stock for making soups and gravies."

2½	*to 3 pounds whole chicken*
4	*tablespoons butter*
1	*tablespoon kosher salt*
1	*celery stalk, chopped*
6	*cups water*

Cut up the chicken into two legs, two breasts, backbone, and wings. Sauté the chicken in the butter and salt to taste over medium heat until golden brown, 10 minutes per side. Add the celery. Turn the heat to low and simmer for 2 minutes. Add the water. Cook over low heat for 30 to 40 minutes. Pull out the chicken and celery and strain the broth. Pick the chicken from the bones for soup meat.

MAKES 4 CUPS

Michael Maxwell

New to the Loveless Cafe but a longtime business partner and friend of Tom Morales, Michael Maxwell describes himself as the food guy. "It's my job to make sure it is the quality and taste we want."

Michael worked with Tom for fifteen years at TomKats and started his own "Home on the Range" catering company as well as a restaurant in Oklahoma called Chino's Bar and Grill. "We served the best barbecue in Oklahoma!" he proclaims.

Michael credits Tom with much of his own barbecue expertise, such as knowing whether or not a pork butt is tender enough by wiggling the blade bone. If it pulls out with ease, the meat is ready. He also says that as a guide in staying true to the spirit of the Loveless, Tom gave him a cookbook by Edna Lewis, who offers cultural logic to her recipes that helps explain why so much southern food is cooked the way it is.

"We had worked together for so long, I knew what Tom was looking for in this place," Michael says. "I came in before opening. We rearranged the equipment, and I worked on the menu. Tom wanted a lot of side dishes. Green beans and yellow squash and hashbrown casserole every day. We wanted to add to the menu, but not change what was good about it." His favorite customer comment after the reopening was from an elderly gentleman who told him, "This is the Loveless Cafe I remember, but with more to offer. It is true to the roots of Nashville and the South."

Michael feels that catering to the movie industry is a terrific school for running a restaurant. "Tom understood 'family style' having grown up in a family of ten," he says. "It was natural to take that to a movie set where the different steps of preparing, cooking, and serving are not separated out. You learn everything, which means you know how a kitchen works and you know how a dining room works. Ideally, it is a seamless process."

Years of motion picture catering also taught Maxwell and Morales certain rules of thumb that they have brought to the kitchen of the Loveless. For example, to make the good old standby macaroni and cheese, he offers these tips:

1. Overcook your pasta. That way, it absorbs moisture before you put it in the sauce. Otherwise, it will absorb moisture from the sauce and turn stiff.

2. Use more sauce, less noodle.

3. A little blue cheese does wonders for the flavor.

4. Cayenne pepper goes well with any cheese.

POTATO-LEEK SOUP

Fresh leeks are the essential ingredient for what Tom calls "a seasonal soup, for the fall when the crops are ripe and ready."

2	pounds leeks
1	stick (¼ pound) plus 6 tablespoons butter
1	tablespoon all-purpose flour
6	cups chicken stock
4	pounds potatoes, peeled and diced
	Salt and pepper

Trim the leeks and wash with cold water, being careful to wash away the dirt deep in the tops. Slice the leeks in half lengthwise and chop into 1-inch pieces. In a large stockpot melt the 6 tablespoons butter and cook the leeks on medium-low heat until tender. Sprinkle the flour over the leeks. Cook for 2 minutes. Increase the heat to high and stir in the chicken stock. Add the potatoes and bring to a boil. Reduce the heat to medium-low and simmer until the potatoes are tender. Season with the salt and pepper to taste. Add the remaining 1 stick of butter before serving.

MAKES 6 TO 8 SERVINGS

Variation: For more substance, add a pound of Andouille sausage and white beans. Add the sausage with the potatoes. Soak the beans overnight, boil them until al dente, 30 minutes, and add with the potatoes, too.

OYSTER STEW

The beautiful thing about middle Tennessee is that you are a close drive to the Gulf Coast or to the Atlantic," Tom says, describing oyster stew as a dish inspired by visits to the Gulf.

1	yellow onion, finely diced
4	plus 4 tablespoons (1 stick) butter
3	tablespoons all-purpose flour
5	cups heated milk
2	cups heavy cream
3	ounces fresh oysters with liquor
1	teaspoon kosher salt
	Pinch of black pepper
	Pinch of cayenne
	Sherry

Sauté the diced onions in 4 tablespoons butter over medium heat until translucent and tender. Sprinkle the flour over the sautéed onions and cook for 2 minutes. Add the heated milk, heavy cream, and oyster liquor. Bring to a simmering boil. In a separate pan, sauté the oysters in the remaining 4 tablespoons butter, salt, and pepper until they begin to curl around the edges. Then add the oysters to the onions and milk mixture and add the cayenne. Add the sherry to taste. Serve hot.

MAKES 6 SERVINGS

CHICKEN & DUMPLINGS

On the subject of dumplings, Tom's enthusiasm is boundless.

"Here's the controversy," he explains: "Is a dumpling a scoop or a strip? For traditionalists like my kid's great grandmother, if she gets a dough scoop, it's *not* chicken and dumplings. She insists on strips. For her, chicken and dumplings begins with broth and all-white meat. Bring it to a slow boil and then lay your dough strips on top. That part is a science, because if you don't have the right amount of flour in the strip, it won't hold up as intended. It takes a lot of time to make the ribbons right. The scoop is easier because you don't have to roll it out. However, with scoops, you run the risk of dumplings that are gooey. I'll sit there with my wife and her mother and her mother's mother, three generations and they'll argue about how to make those dumplings.

"The secret of good dumplings is to have stock at a slow boil, not a fast one. Too fast and you end up with a gooey ball inside."

1	*(3-pound) chicken, washed and trimmed*
4	*cups chicken stock*
2	*tablespoons butter*
1	*tablespoon black pepper*
	Salt
¼	*(20-ounce) box Bisquick mix*
2	*tablespoons chopped parsley*

Place the chicken and enough water to cover into a stockpot and bring to a simmer. Poach the chicken until just done, about 30 minutes. Set aside to cool. When the chicken has cooled, pull the white meat only into bite-size pieces. Place the pulled chicken back into the water and add the chicken stock, butter, and black pepper. Add the salt to taste. (Salt is not always necessary, since the chicken stock tends to be on the salty side.)

Mix the Bisquick according to the box recipe for dumplings. This can be made ahead of time and refrigerated up to 2 days. Use an ice cream scoop to make dumplings, or roll out the dough to ¼-inch thickness and cut into strips the length of the pot's diameter. Drop the dough scoops or strips into the stock with the chicken and cook until done, 10 to 12 minutes on simmer. Sprinkle the parsley over the top. Serve immediately.

MAKES 4 TO 6 SERVINGS

ROASTED BUTTERNUT SQUASH SOUP WITH CORNBREAD CROUTONS

Although so much of the cooking on which Tom Morales grew up was seasonal, there are many dishes designed to be made when seasonal produce is not available.

"Butternut squash is a vegetable that will hold for a long time and still be good. You can still have it at Christmas, even if it was harvested in fall."

Soup

2	tablespoons butter
1	butternut squash, cut in half lengthwise
6	Roma tomatoes, sliced
4	garlic cloves
2	plus 2 tablespoons olive oil
1	tablespoon balsamic vinegar
1	cup diced red onion
½	cup diced carrots
½	cup diced celery
6	cups chicken stock
	Salt and black pepper
¼	cup fresh thyme
2	tablespoons chopped fresh parsley
2	tablespoons chopped green onion
1	tablespoon fresh sage
1	tablespoon butter
	Fresh herbs (such as sage or thyme or parsley) for garnish

Cornbread croutons

4	cups cornbread (fresh or day-old), cut into 4-inch cubes
4	tablespoons butter
2	tablespoons olive oil
1	tablespoon salt
½	tablespoon black pepper

Preheat the oven to 350°F. Place 1 tablespoon butter in each squash half. Roast the butternut squash on a baking pan for 35 to 40 minutes or until soft to the touch. Toss the tomatoes and garlic with 2 tablespoons of the olive oil and the balsamic vinegar and roast them on a baking pan for 30 minutes. Heat the remaining 2 tablespoons of olive oil in a large saucepan over medium-high heat. Sauté the onion, carrots, and celery until tender. Add the chicken stock and salt and pepper to taste. Simmer for 20 minutes. Remove the meat of the squash with a spoon and put it into the soup. Simmer for 20 minutes. Add the thyme, parsley, green onion, sage, and butter. Let cool. Process in a food processor until smooth.

To make the croutons, toss the cornbread cubes in a mixture of the butter, olive oil, salt, and pepper. Arrange the cubes on a greased baking sheet and broil for 15 to 20 minutes or until golden brown. Pour the soup back into the saucepan over medium heat until warm. Garnish the soup with the cornbread croutons and fresh herbs. Serve hot.

MAKES 6 TO 8 SERVINGS

CRAWFISH BISQUE

Tom attributes crawfish bisque to the boatmen who returned north up the Natchez Trace from New Orleans. "There's a lot of connection to history here," he says. "They brought back spices as well as cooking ideas."

1¼	cups diced yellow onion
¾	cup diced red bell pepper
1	cup diced celery
2	tablespoons chopped garlic
⅓	cup seafood base
1	bunch thyme (10 ounces), stems removed
	Dash of paprika
1	to 2 teaspoons Tabasco
8	cups (½ gallon) water
2	to 2½ cups heavy cream
1	pound crawfish tails, whole
4	tablespoons canola oil
4	tablespoons all-purpose flour
⅓	cup sherry

Place the onion, bell pepper, celery, garlic, seafood base, thyme, paprika, Tabasco, and water in a pot and simmer for about 20 minutes. Add the cream and crawfish tails and then return to a simmer. In a skillet heat the oil over medium and mix in the flour and cook until thick and smooth. Thicken the crawfish mixture with the roux as needed, and cook until the "starchy" taste is gone. Remove the crawfish from the heat and add the sherry.

MAKES 8 SERVINGS

Main
Dishes

Country Ham

Pulled Pork

Beef Hash

Pot Roast

Barbecued Ribs

Smoking Pork Loin

Braised Pork Chops

Fried Pork Chops

Fried Chicken

Grilled Chicken Breasts
with Blackstrap Molasses

Fried Green Tomato BLT

Country-Fried Steak

Pepper Steak

Suppertime Beef Casserole

Meatloaf

Creamed Chicken with Fresh Mushrooms

Turkey & Carol Faye's Biscuit and
Cornbread Stuffing

Grilled Doves

Roasted Wild Duck

Pan-Fried Trout

Fried Catfish

COUNTRY HAM

Ham debates are common among southern food aficionados.

"Who does it best? Who does it right?" Tom queries. He explains the basic differences:

Virginia hams, which are salt cured, were the first. In more mountainous regions, they used smoke to keep flies away, and that has become part of the curing process in middle Tennessee: less salt and more smoke. The old-timers tell me that the smoke method makes a more tender ham, and a less salty one. Most Virginia hams need to be soaked in the bathtub overnight. It would be sacrilegious to soak a Tennessee ham.

---

4   *(¼-inch thick) bone-in center cut country ham slices*
      (can be purchased through www.lovelesscafe.com)

2   *tablespoons butter*

Rinse the steaks with water and pat dry. Heat the butter in large cast-iron skillet or frying pan over medium-high heat. Cook the steaks approximately 3 to 4 minutes each side. At this time, remove steaks. You may make Red-Eye Gravy (see page 82) in the pan at this time using the drippings from the fried ham steaks.

MAKES 4 SERVINGS

PULLED PORK

While all southern food and cooking traditions interest Tom Morales, barbecue is his special passion. "It is something that everybody takes pride in," he says. "And every cook thinks his or hers is the very best. Therein lies the reason I love to try every barbecue I come across. To this day, I still find people with techniques that make me curious to find out how they do what they do. The one thing about which I am adamant is hickory wood. No one can convince me that red oak or black oak or mesquite works as well as hickory. Mesquite is fine on beef or steak. Apple wood is fine for smoked fish. But for pork, hickory is essential."

8   to 10 pounds Boston butt or pork shoulder
     Loveless Dry Rub (see page 88)

Liberally coat the pork with the dry rub mixture. Start your grill or smoker (real charcoal is preferred). Also, you should soak hickory chips overnight before beginning this procedure. Place your charcoal grates at the lowest setting and your food rack at the highest setting. If using a gas grill, light just one side. If using a charcoal grill, move all the charcoal to one side. Place the shoulder on the cold side, fat side up. Add hickory chips to the fire and close the lid. Add more chips every 20 to 30 minutes. Add charcoal as needed (don't let fire die). Continue to smoke the pork for 6 hours. Wrap the roast with heavy-duty aluminum foil and slow cook for 3 more hours. Remove from the heat and "pull" the meat. *"Pulling"* pork means to separate the meat from the fat and gristle. Toss the meat with a vinegar hot sauce. Serve with barbecue sauce, and top with coleslaw on a hoe cake or hamburger bun.

MAKES 6 TO 8 SERVINGS

Note: If you prefer a crisp outer skin, do not wrap the pork before flipping it for the final 3 hours of cooking.

BEEF HASH

Beef hash is a way to use leftover beef or to make the most out of a cheap cut. The general idea is to cook the meat until it literally falls apart. Then you add onions and potatoes and you have a hash suitable for a sandwich or as a breakfast meat in place of bacon or ham.

2   *pounds beef (leftovers are fine)*

1   *tablespoon salt*

1   *tablespoon black pepper*

2   *Idaho potatoes, diced*

1   *large yellow sweet onion, chopped*

Place the beef in a stockpot. Cover with water and bring to a boil. Reduce the heat to medium-low. Add the salt and pepper, cover, and simmer for 2 hours or until the meat is tender and falling apart. Add the potatoes and onions, and additional water if needed, and return to a boil. Reduce the heat and simmer, uncovered, for 30 minutes or until the liquid has evaporated. The beef can be eaten hot or cold and it makes a great sandwich.

MAKES 6 TO 8 SERVINGS

George Harvell

I am the smoke guy," says George Harvell, who arrives at the Loveless barbecue pit each morning between 2 A.M. and 4 A.M. He pulls well-wrapped and falling-apart-tender hunks of brisket and pork shoulder from the dying embers, shovels out the pit, and refires the hickory wood to begin to slow-smoke the day's meats.

Harvell started in the foodservice business at the estimable Belle Meade Cafeteria back in the late 1970s ultimately becoming a private chef. "I wasn't too busy at first, so I played a lot of basketball at the YMCA. There I met Tom Morales, who had just started TomKats with his wife Kathie. They weren't busy, either, so Tom and I played a lot of basketball together."

Harvell hired on with TomKats, first doing piecework, then doing just about everything, including catering twenty-nine movies and being chef at the Starwood Amphitheater. During ten years with TomKats, he learned the art of barbecue, an art about which he has some very definite opinions. He was so enamored of the subject that he decided to open his own barbecue business when he left TomKats. He went to Tom Morales to see if his old boss happened to have an unneeded grill he could buy. When Morales described his plans for the Loveless, he included a description of the new smokehouse he was planning to build. "He hired me," Harvell recalls, "and he told me they were building that smokehouse pretty much for me."

Foremost among Harvell's absolute rules of barbecue is the importance of hickory wood. Harvell starts his fire with seasoned hickory logs, then adds green ones for more smoke. He also throws in water-soaked hickory chips if he needs to bring down the flames and/or bring up the flavor. "That's the true art of barbecue," he declares. "The right balance between heat and smoke. That and a good dry rub."

Randy Williams

Randy Williams, general manager of the Loveless Cafe, grew up in the food service business. From the time he was eight years old, his father ran Nashville's Cabin Restaurant, a breakfast and lunch place that specialized in homemade buttermilk biscuits, country ham, and such blue plate specials as barbecue pork and beef stew. "He was a chef and a master baker," Williams recalls. "He made the biscuits and he taught me how to make biscuits. Of course, Loveless biscuits are a trademark, a little different than what I'm used to, and something we could never change."

After attending the Culinary Institute of America, Williams joined up with TomKats, where he avows he got the best education in the world for running a restaurant. "In the catering business, you learn to think on your feet," he says. "You have to be very organized, you have to make split second decisions and constantly adjust to changing situations. And you have to be more personalized in your service, which adds an extra touch to the rest biz."

He is now concentrating on the front of the house at the Loveless Cafe and making sure it runs the way it should: the managers, the greeters, and the servers. He is also working on recipe development and overseeing the kitchen. Part of that plan is to expand the menu. Of course, the trademark ham, fried chicken, biscuits, and preserves will always be the anchors, but Williams anticipates adding vegetable dishes that reflect seasonal produce and regional farm bounty and daily specials that give Nashville locals reasons to return to the Loveless again and again.

POT ROAST

Tom jokingly refers to pot roast as "wintertime barbecue" because it is beef that you cook very slowly, but indoors in a pot instead of outdoors in a smoke pit.

¼	cup canola oil
4	pounds shoulder roast or bottom round, trimmed and sliced into 2 pieces
2	tablespoons Montreal seasoning or salt and pepper
¼	cup all-purpose flour
1½	gallons water
4	carrots, sliced 1 inch thick
2	large yellow onions, sliced ¾ inch thick
2	celery stalks, sliced 1 inch thick

In a skillet heat the oil over medium-high heat. Rub the roast or bottom round with the seasoning and sprinkle with enough flour to coat. Place the roast or bottom round in the hot oil and brown on both sides, about 5 minutes per side. Remove the beef and set it aside. Add the remaining flour (about 2 tablespoons) to the oil to make a roux, stirring until the roux is brown. Place the beef in a large pot (twice the volume of the beef). Add the roux and enough water to cover. Simmer, covered, for 1 hour, adding more water as necessary. When the beef is tender and falling apart, add the carrots, onion, and celery and continue cooking, covered, for 30 more minutes. Add salt and pepper to taste before serving.

MAKES 8 TO 12 SERVINGS

BARBECUED RIBS

"From Kansas City to St. Louis to Memphis to Nashville to the Carolinas, everybody has a different way of cooking ribs," says Tom, who used to operate a barbecue restaurant of his own in South Carolina. "Our method is slow-smoke, indirect heat. We like to use the fattiest ribs; the fat cooks out, but it makes the rib tender and infuses the meat with flavor. The test of a rib's doneness is when you can pull it apart but the meat stays on the bone. If the bone pulls completely out of the meat, it is overdone."

---

2   *slabs baby back ribs or 1 slab spare ribs (about 15 ribs)*
      Loveless Dry Rub (see page 88)

Liberally coat the ribs with the dry rub mixture. Light your grill or smoker. Real charcoal is preferable. Use hickory chips that have been soaked in water overnight. Set the charcoal grates at the lowest setting and the food grates at the highest setting. If using a gas grill, light only one side. If using charcoal, move all the coals to one side. Place the ribs on the cold side. Add the chips. Close the lid. Smoke for 1 hour. Turn the ribs. Smoke for 1 more hour. Remember: Don't let the fire die. Add charcoal as needed. Add hickory chips every 20 to 30 minutes. You have three options at this point. You can 1) wrap the ribs with heavy-duty aluminum foil and cook another 45 minutes to an hour or 2) you can brush the ribs with barbecue sauce and cook 45 minutes to an hour longer or 3) you can pull the ribs and serve them dry rubbed Memphis-style and serve the sauce on the side.

MAKES 4 TO 6 SERVINGS

SMOKING PORK LOIN

Good for any size pork loin. Pork loin can also be cut into your favorite chop size and smoked.

	Wet Brine (see page 87)
2	*to 3 pounds pork loin*
	Loveless Dry Rub (see page 88)
	Loveless Peach Preserves (see page 54)

Brine the pork for a day before cooking. Brining guarantees moist and flavored meat. Season the pork loin with the dry rub. Light your grill or smoker. Real charcoal is preferable. Use hickory chips that have been soaked in water overnight. Set the charcoal grates at the lowest setting and the food grates at the highest setting. If using a gas grill, light only one side. If using charcoal, move all the coals to one side. Place the pork loin on the cold side. Add the chips. Close the lid. Smoke for 1 hour. Turn the pork loin and smoke for 1 more hour. Don't let the fire die. Add hickory chips as needed; check every 20 to 30 minutes. Smoke until the meat reaches 130°F. Remove the pork and cut into ¼-inch chops. Cook the cut chops directly over the heat, basting with the peach preserves, and cook until the meat reaches 145°F.

MAKES 6 TO 8 SERVINGS

BRAISED PORK CHOPS

When I grew up, *braised* was another term for tender," Tom notes. This is a way of slow-cooking pork chops until they are ready to fall apart.

6	(6-ounce) center cut pork chops
¼	cup canola
⅓	cup water
1	tablespoon prepared mustard
1	tablespoon vinegar
1	tablespoon brown sugar
1	tablespoon Worcestershire or soy sauce
1	teaspoon garlic salt

Trim the fat from the chops. Heat the oil in a skillet over medium-high heat. Brown the chops and sprinkle with salt. Mix the water, mustard, vinegar, brown sugar, Worcestershire sauce, and garlic salt to make a sauce to cover the chops. Cover and simmer 1 hour or until very tender. Remove the lid and cook the sauce until thick.

MAKES 6 SERVINGS

FRIED PORK CHOPS

Tom only half-jokingly describes the three staples of a true southern diet as 1) fried pork chops, 2) fried chicken, and 3) country-fried steak. "They are all basically prepared the same way," he says. "The key things are a cast-iron skillet, and not to cover the meat with the oil."

½	cup all-purpose flour
2	tablespoons salt
1	tablespoon black pepper
½	to 1 cup canola oil
8	thin-cut, breakfast-style pork chops
1	tablespoon granulated garlic (optional)

Mix the flour, salt, and black pepper in a plastic bag and shake to combine. Pour it out onto a plate. Heat the oil in cast-iron skillet over medium heat. Make sure the oil just barely covers the bottom of skillet. It is important that the oil is hot but not smoking. Dredge the pork chops in the flour mixture and cook them in the skillet until browned on both sides, about 5 minutes per side. (You may need to add more oil during the cooking process. Never submerge the meat in oil.) Place the cooked pork chops on a drain rack or unbleached paper (i.e. brown paper bag) to drain. Serve immediately when all done.

MAKES 4 (2-CHOP) SERVINGS

Linda Furlow

A second-generation employee of the Loveless Cafe, Linda Furlow came to the restaurant because many years ago her mother worked here with Carol Fay Ellison. Carol Fay subsequently imparted to Linda the biscuit recipe and now when Carol Fay is off, it is Linda who makes the biscuits. "I am sure an expert could tell the difference between her biscuits and mine," Linda suggests. "The recipe is the same, but everyone has a touch."

When she is not making biscuits, Linda's field of operations is the flat top where pancakes are flipped and country ham is sizzled every day starting at six in the morning. The proper timing of how meals get plated means that working at the grill is a high-pressure place in the kitchen, but according to VP of Operations, Jesse Goldstein, Linda is "one of the toughest line cooks there is."

FRIED CHICKEN

Martha White self-rising flour is a staple in all Southern pantries and the basis for the breading used on Loveless fried chicken. According to Tom, "The breading is what made Loveless fried chicken famous, and the frying technique is critical too."

2	*fryer chickens (3 pounds or less), cut up*

Fried chicken flour

1¾	*cups self-rising flour*
2	*tablespoons Loveless Seasoned Salt (see page 88)*
1	*teaspoon black pepper*
2½	*teaspoons garlic powder*

Cut the chickens into eighths. Rinse them in cold water and then let them soak in fresh cold salted water for at least 30 minutes. Drain and pat them dry.

Mix thoroughly the flour, seasoned salt, pepper, and garlic powder to make the fried chicken flour. Heat an inch of vegetable oil in a large skillet over medium-high heat (375°F in an electric skillet). Dredge the chicken through the flour mixture, coating well on both sides. Place the chicken in the hot oil, making sure the chicken pieces aren't touching each other. When the chicken is browned, about 5 minutes, turn the pieces over and reduce the heat to medium (300°F), cover, and cook for 20 minutes. Then, remove the lid, bring the heat back to medium high and turn the chicken, cooking an additional 5 to 7 minutes. Let the chicken drain on paper towels before eating.

MAKES ENOUGH FOR 3½ POUNDS CHICKEN

GRILLED CHICKEN BREASTS WITH BLACKSTRAP MOLASSES

Blackstrap molasses glaze is an alternative to barbecue sauce: sweeter and more intense.

4	to 6 (5-ounce) chicken breasts (with skin on)
8	cups Wet Brine (see page 87)
1	tablespoon salt
1	tablespoon black pepper
1	tablespoon granulated garlic
1	cup Backstrap Molasses Glaze (see page 86)

Place the chicken in the brine at least 2 hours before cooking. Mix the salt, pepper, and granulated garlic in a small bowl or Ziploc bag. Start a charcoal grill or preheat the broiler. When the coals are white hot, remove the chicken from the brine and place them skin side down on the grill. When the chicken starts to cook and the fat produces flames, rotate the chicken on the grill a half-turn, keeping the skin side down for an additional 2 to 3 minutes, careful not to let the flames burn the chicken. When the skin side is browned, flip the chicken over and put the glaze on the skin side. Cook the opposite side 3 to 5 minutes, again careful not to burn. Return to the glazed skin side for 1 minute while glazing the top. Remove and serve immediately.

MAKES 4 TO 6 SERVINGS

FRIED GREEN TOMATO BLT

We did this one because people love fried green tomatoes," Tom says. "It is a twist on a traditional BLT."

1	to 4 green tomatoes, sliced
	Salt and black pepper
1	cup yellow cornmeal
1	cup canola oil
3	tablespoons mayonnaise
2	slices toasted wheat-berry bread
2	to 3 lettuce leaves
3	to 4 cooked bacon strips

Season the sliced tomatoes with salt and pepper to taste and dredge them in the cornmeal. Heat the oil in a skillet over medium-high heat. Fry the tomatoes until golden brown on both sides. Spread the mayonnaise on the bread. Add the lettuce on both sides. Add the fried green tomatoes and bacon. Build a sandwich and cut in half.

MAKES 1 SANDWICH

COUNTRY-FRIED STEAK

W hen cooking country-fried steak, all the debris that remains in the bottom of the skillet once the meat is removed is essential for making pan gravy. And the gravy is vital for the mashed potatoes that southern culinary law declares must accompany country-fried steak— or fried chicken or pork chops.

1	*tablespoon granulated garlic*
½	*cup all-purpose flour*
2	*tablespoons salt*
1	*tablespoon black pepper*
½	*to 1 cup canola oil*
4	*tenderized steak cutlets or cube steaks*

Mix the garlic, flour, salt, and black pepper in a plastic bag and shake to combine. Pour it out onto a plate. Heat the oil in a cast-iron skillet over medium heat. Make sure that the oil just barely covers the bottom of the skillet. It is important that oil is hot but not smoking. Dredge the steak cutlets in the flour mixture and cook in the skillet until browned on both sides, about 5 minutes per side, depending on desired doneness. (You may need to add more oil during the cooking process. Never submerge meat in oil.) Place the cooked chops on a drain rack or unbleached paper (i.e., brown paper bag) to drain. Serve immediately when all done.

MAKES 4 SERVINGS

PEPPER STEAK

My first thought of pepper steak is how the aroma fills up the kitchen," Tom says. "For us, this recipe is a way to take a cheap piece of steak and give it flavor. But you can upgrade the steak to a better cut and it's great, too."

½	cup chopped onion
2	green bell peppers, cut into strips
½	cup (1 stick) butter
2	pounds round steak, cut into 8 pieces
⅛	teaspoon garlic powder
1	(16-ounce) can chopped tomatoes
1	beef bouillon cube, crushed
1	teaspoon cornstarch
¼	cup water
3	tablespoons soy sauce
1	teaspoon sugar
1	teaspoon salt

Sauté the onion and green peppers in the butter in a large skillet over medium-high heat for 2 minutes or until the vegetables are tender; drain. Remove the vegetables to a bowl. Arrange the meat in the pan drippings in the skillet. Sprinkle with the garlic powder. Cook until the meat is brown on both sides, about 5 minutes per side. Combine the tomatoes and crushed bouillon and pour over the meat. Bring to a boil, reduce the heat to medium low, and simmer for 10 minutes. Whisk together the cornstarch, water, soy sauce, sugar, and salt and add to the tomato mixture. Cook until the tomato mixture is thickened and the meat is tender. Stir in the onion and green peppers and cook for 2 to 3 more minutes.

MAKES 8 SERVINGS

SUPPERTIME BEEF CASSEROLE

Like so many casseroles, this one is a way to use leftovers and to extend the main ingredient if you don't have much of it. Tom recalls coming home from school and popping this casserole into the oven after it had been prepared the day before.

1   (7-ounce) package macaroni and cheese
1   pound ground beef
1   garlic clove, chopped
1   (10-ounce) can onion soup
     Salt and pepper

Preheat the oven to 350°F. Prepare the macaroni and cheese according to the package directions. Brown the ground beef with the garlic in a skillet over medium heat, stirring until the ground beef is crumbly; drain. Add the soup and prepared macaroni and cheese; mix well. Season with the salt and pepper to taste. Spoon the mixture into a 2-quart casserole. Bake for 30 minutes.

MAKES 4 SERVINGS

Note: You may substitute garlic powder for the fresh garlic.

MEATLOAF

Tom recalls, "Having grown up in a large family, I came to realize that meatloaf was a way of extending the limited amount of ground meat we had by adding oats or breadcrumbs. This was another thrifty dish."

½	cup diced onions
2	tablespoons granulated garlic
1	tablespoon oil
2	pounds ground beef
2	tablespoons Loveless Seasoned Salt (see page 88)
2	tablespoons black pepper
1	(8-ounce) can diced tomatoes
½	cup steak sauce
4	eggs, beaten
1	tablespoon chopped garlic
½	cup dried oats

Preheat the oven to 350°F. Sauté the onions and granulated garlic in the oil over medium heat. Put in a mixing bowl to cool. Add the ground beef, seasoned salt, pepper, tomatoes, steak sauce, eggs, chopped garlic, and oats and mix well. Mold the mixture into a loaf shape, place in a loaf pan, and bake for 1 hour. Loveless Barbecue Sauce (page 80) on top gives added flavor.

MAKES 4 TO 6 SERVINGS

CREAMED CHICKEN WITH FRESH MUSHROOMS

When entertaining large numbers of people, creamed chicken is a great one-pot meal. You can serve it over biscuits, toast, rice, or pasta.

1	*(3-pound) chicken*
1	*(16-ounce) package sliced fresh mushrooms*
1	*tablespoon butter*
½	*cup milk*
2	*tablespoons all-purpose flour*
¼	*teaspoon curry powder (or to taste)*

Rinse the chicken. Place the chicken in a saucepan and cover with water. Cook over medium-high heat until tender, 30 to 45 minutes; drain, reserving the broth. Chop the chicken, discarding the skin and bones. Sauté the mushrooms in the butter in a large skillet over medium-high heat; drain. Transfer the mushrooms to a small bowl. Mix the milk and flour together and combine with the reserved broth in the skillet. Cook over medium heat until thickened, stirring constantly. Add the chicken and mushrooms. Season with the curry powder. Cook until heated through, about 10 minutes. Serve over cooked rice or egg bread.

MAKES 4 TO 5 SERVINGS

TURKEY & CAROL FAY'S BISCUIT AND CORNBREAD STUFFING

Very few southerners violate the customs of Thanksgiving," Tom observes. "This is a set meal for the holiday. While we might serve Cornish game hens at an upscale restaurant, turkey is tradition."

Turkey

1	(18-pound) turkey
1	medium onion, chopped
3	celery stalks, chopped
2	quarts water
	Poultry seasoning
	Pepper

Carol Fay's Biscuit and Cornbread Stuffin'

1	(16-ounce) box Jiffy cornbread mix

1	pound biscuits (can be fresh or leftovers)
1	cup (2 sticks) butter
1	yellow onion, diced
3	celery stalks, diced
2	tablespoons rubbed sage
½	cup chicken or turkey stock
1	tablespoon poultry seasoning
	Salt
1	tablespoon black pepper

Rinse the turkey and place in a large roasting pan. Add the chopped onion and celery. Pour the water over the top. Sprinkle the turkey with poultry seasoning and pepper to taste. Preheat the oven to 325°F.

Prepare the cornbread according to the package's directions. Bake to internal temperature of 160°F. Remove from oven and allow to cool 20 minutes before slicing. Cut the cornbread and biscuits into cubes or crumble into pieces and place in a large mixing bowl. Heat the butter in a large skillet over medium heat. Add the onion, celery, and sage and sauté until the onion is translucent, about 5 minutes. Add the sautéed vegetables to the cornbread and biscuits. Add the chicken or turkey stock and combine. Add the poultry seasoning, salt to taste, and pepper. Pour the mixture into a large baking dish and bake until the top is light brown with a touch of crust, about 20 minutes. For a drier stuffing bake it uncovered; for a moist stuffing cover with aluminum foil while baking.

MAKES 15 TO 20 SERVINGS

Note: Carol Fay says it works great with leftover biscuits and cornbread.

GRILLED DOVES

Local hunters frequently came to the Loveless kitchen asking the cooks to prepare the birds they bagged.

---

4   *medium doves, cleaned and dressed*
½   *cup orange juice*
½   *cup Italian dressing*
      Partially cooked bacon strips

Marinate the doves in the orange juice mixed with the Italian dressing for 3 to 4 hours. Drain and dry on paper towels. Wrap the bacon around each dove and secure with toothpicks. Allow to sit for 20 to 30 minutes. Grill on low heat until done, about 30 minutes.

MAKES 4 SERVINGS

ROASTED WILD DUCK

Southerners are hunters," Tom says. "Duck is late fall, early winter game. Like the dove, it has always been a way to supplement your meat ration. If you shoot it, you eat it: that's the rule. People always looked forward to hunting season because it meant the menu would change."

2	*whole ducks, cleaned and dressed*
2	*tablespoons salt*
2	*teaspoons baking soda*
4	*small apples, cored and sliced*
	Salt and pepper
2	*tablespoons vinegar*
2	*cups water*
½	*cup sherry wine (optional)*
4	*tablespoons butter*

Soak the cleaned ducks in cold, salt water for 1 hour (about 2 tablespoons salt per quart). Wash well and drain. Fill the pot with clean water and add the baking soda (2 teaspoons per quart). Boil the ducks in the soda water for 10 minutes. Remove and wash well. Preheat the oven to 250°F. Put an apple inside of each duck, and season inside and out with salt and pepper. Place the ducks in a covered roaster. Pour 1 tablespoon vinegar over each duck. Add the water and cook for 3 to 4 hours or until tender. If desired, the ducks may be basted with sherry wine the last 2 hours of cooking. Uncover the last 30 minutes, put 2 tablespoons butter on each duck, and brown. The gravy from the ducks is delicious with rice.

MAKES 4 TO 6 SERVINGS, DEPENDING ON THE SIZE OF THE DUCKS

PAN-FRIED TROUT

Pan-fried trout made it onto our menu because it is raised locally," Tom explains. "We like to use fresh local ingredients; and in this case, we tried to push the boundary by adding pecan pieces in the breading. And we add pepper relish to the tartar sauce. It has turned out to be extremely popular. It is a serious plate of food with a lot of plate coverage, a good-size dinner.

4	*medium fresh trout fillets, cleaned and trimmed*
1	*cup fried chicken flour (see page 118)*
1	*cup catfish cornmeal (see page 132)*
1	*cup pecan pieces*
	Salt and pepper
¼	*cup (½ stick) butter*
¼	*cup canola oil*
1	*lemon*

Wash the trout fillets under cold running water. Dry with a paper towel. Put the seasoned flour, cornmeal, and pecans in a food processor and chop to a medium-fine mixture. Salt and pepper the trout to taste and then press the fillets into the flour mixture. Melt the butter and canola oil in saucepan over medium-high heat. Sauté the trout fillets until golden brown on one side and then turn to brown the other side. Serve with lemon wedges and tartar sauce.

MAKES 4 SERVINGS

Marie Barrett

Waitress Marie Barrett is family. Not really; she isn't blood-related to anyone else at the Loveless Cafe; but she is part of it, and it is part of her in ways that are far more than a mere job opportunity. She came to work here when she was fifteen years old. Her motive? To be near her first boyfriend, grandson of longtime employee Mary Elizabeth Roberts. He was then working as a dishwasher. The kids' relationship ended, but Marie stayed on; and this has been the only place she's ever worked.

"I learned to do pretty much everything," she says. "I've done payroll and schedules, but now I work the dining room." When Marie waits on a table, customers are ensured of the full Loveless experience. With her sorghum-sweet middle Tennessee accent, she can virtually sing the menu that she knows so well, and she can field just about any issue strangers present.

"I get people who have no idea what grits are!" she says with some amazement. "I tell them it's plain ground corn. And there are some who ask if we've got regular ham because they think that all country ham is so terribly salty. But I recommend our country ham even to first-timers. It's salty, but not too; and it is so good!"

As one who felt very much part of a cherished tradition, Marie grew apprehensive back in 2003 when it became known that the McCabe family would be selling the restaurant and a new owner, Tom Morales, would be making changes. She wasn't the only one concerned. "This was Donna McCabe's baby," Marie says. "She wanted to make sure it was going to thrive. And I can't tell you how many customers I had back then who were so worried about what might happen to their favorite restaurant. We were all worried. But he promised that the important things wouldn't change."

As it turned out, the temporary closing was a special blessing for Marie, who gave birth just two weeks after the door was shut for renovations in February 2004. That gave her four months to stay home with her new daughter, Brooke. Still, anxiety about the new regime remained. "He was bigger than what I'd ever known," Marie says, referring to Tom Morales' work as a caterer for large-scale Hollywood productions. "But he kept his promise. He saved the Loveless. And now I am so proud and happy to be back."

FRIED CATFISH

Cooking catfish is a tradition that has been passed down through generations. This breading combines both flour and cornmeal, and can be used for almost any kind of fish fry.

Catfish cornmeal

1½	cups yellow cornmeal
2½	cups fried chicken flour (see page 118)
1	tablespoon salt
1	tablespoon black pepper
1	tablespoon Loveless Seasoned Salt (see page 88)
1	tablespoon dry mustard
1	tablespoon lemon pepper
½	cup canola oil
3	eggs, beaten
6	to 8 (4-ounce) catfish fillets

Mix thoroughly the cornmeal, flour, salt, pepper, seasoned salt, dry mustard, and lemon pepper in a large mixing bowl or plastic bag. Pour into a shallow pie plate or baking dish. Preheat a large skillet over medium-high heat with the oil. Put the eggs in another shallow baking dish and whisk in 3 to 4 tablespoons of water. Dredge the catfish fillets in the egg wash and then press into the catfish cornmeal on both sides. Drop into the hot skillet and fry on both sides until done, about 5 minutes per side.

MAKES 6 TO 8 SERVINGS

Side Dishes

Hush Puppies

Macaroni & Cheese

Mashed Potatoes

Cheesy Potatoes

Caramelized Sweet Potatoes

White Beans

Black-Eyed Pea Cakes

Donna's Broccoli & Rice

Broccoli Chicken Casserole

Squash Casserole

Yellow Squash

Southern Greens

Grilled Zucchini, Onions & Red Peppers

Cream Corn

Fried Corn

Cornbread Dressing

Lib's Chow- Chow

Green Tomato Chow-Chow

Sweet Potato Casserole

Corn & Potato Gratin

Black-Eyed Peas

HUSH PUPPIES

Tom believes that the secret of a good hush puppy is a crusty outside and a tender inside. How do you get that?

"It depends entirely on the temperature of the oil," he asserts. "If it's too hot, you get mush on the inside. It needs to be cooked, but not hard through and through. If the grease is smoking, you are way too hot."

2	*cups cornmeal*
2	*tablespoons all-purpose flour*
1	*teaspoon baking soda*
1	*teaspoon baking powder*
1	*teaspoon kosher salt*
½	*cup grated onion*
¼	*cup sliced green onion*
1	*egg yolk*
1	*cup buttermilk*
1½	*to 2 cups egg whites (about 8 eggs)*

Mix together the cornmeal, flour, baking soda, baking powder, and salt. Add the grated onion and sliced green onions. Take the egg yolk and buttermilk and blend into the batter. Whip the egg whites into stiff peaks. Fold the egg whites into the batter and drop by the teaspoonful into the deep fry. Cook until golden brown.

MAKES 6 TO 8 SERVINGS

MACARONI & CHEESE

W*hy is macaroni and cheese always around?* Tom wondered. He asked his mama and she said, "So children will always get their fill."

2	*pounds elbow macaroni*
1	*tablespoon salt*
¼	*cup canola oil*
¼	*cup all-purpose flour*
½	*gallon milk*
½	*tablespoon cayenne*
¼	*tablespoon white pepper*
¼	*pound (about 1 cup) blue cheese crumbles*
¼	*pound (about 1 cup) shredded Cheddar cheese*
1	*pound (about 3 cups) Velveeta cheese*

Preheat the oven to 375°F. Cook the elbow macaroni in a stockpot of boiling water with the salt. Cook the macaroni until limp, not al dente. Pour the macaroni into a large rectangle baking dish. In a heavy saucepan heat the oil over medium heat. Add the flour and stir to make a roux, bringing to a light simmer, being careful not to scorch the flour. Heat the milk in another heavy-bottom pan over medium heat and add the roux, cooking out the roux to make a thickened sauce. Add the cayenne, white pepper, blue cheese, Cheddar cheese, and Velveeta. Blend well and pour over the macaroni and mix well. Cook for 5 to 10 minutes in the oven.

MAKES 6 TO 8 SERVINGS

Note: Rule of thumb: more sauce, less macaroni.

MASHED POTATOES

Three staples of the southern kitchen absolutely demand mashed potatoes: country-fried steak, fried pork chops, and fried chicken. As Tom puts it, "Any student of southern cooking knows that anything fried demands mashed potatoes on the side. And the gravy must be made with the debris or drippings of the meat. If you're doing fried chicken, you are doing fried chicken gravy."

He adds a tip about the gravy making: "If you use whole milk, you have to add a little water, or else it gets too thick. And while you want sausage gravy very thick, gravy for mashed potatoes shouldn't be."

4	*pounds whole Idaho potatoes, peeled*
8	*tablespoons butter, melted*
1	*cup half-and-half, warmed (or 1 cup reserved potato water)*
1½	*teaspoons salt*
1½	*teaspoons black pepper*

Place the potatoes in a large cooking pot and cover with cold water. Bring to a boil. Reduce the heat to medium low. Simmer until the potatoes are just tender (20 to 30 minutes). Drain water, reserving 1 cup if desired. Add the melted butter and then add the warmed half-and-half or the 1 cup reserved potato water if desired. Mash with a potato masher until creamy. Add the salt and black pepper.

MAKES 4 TO 6 SERVINGS

CHEESY POTATOES

A variation of potatoes au gratin, but Southern-style thanks to the added bacon.

8	medium new potatoes, not peeled
¾	cup shredded sharp Cheddar cheese
6	slices cooked bacon, crumbled
½	cup (1 stick) butter, melted

Cut the potatoes into bite-size pieces and place in a large saucepan with enough water to cover. Boil until tender, about 10 minutes; drain. Preheat the oven to 350°F. Layer the potatoes and cheese in a 2-quart casserole. Sprinkle with the bacon. Pour the butter evenly over the top. Bake for 10 minutes or until the cheese is melted. Serve hot.

MAKES 6 SERVINGS

CARAMELIZED SWEET POTATOES

The sweet potato is like Forrest Gump and shrimp," Tom says. "You have a bunch of ways to cook them. This is just one variation. When the sweet potatoes are really sweet, you hardly need any sugar at all."

3	large sweet potatoes, peeled and quartered
¼	cup firmly packed brown sugar
1	teaspoon vanilla extract
1	teaspoon pumpkin spice
¼	cup lemon juice

Preheat the oven to 350°F. Place the sweet potatoes in a covered baking dish or casserole dish. Add the brown sugar, vanilla, pumpkin spice, and lemon juice. Bake for 45 minutes to 1 hour until tender.

MAKES 4 TO 6 SERVINGS

WHITE BEANS

Mama has her own way with white beans and pinto beans, which is different than cooking green beans," Tom advises. "She brings them to a boil, drains them, and sets them aside five or ten minutes. Meanwhile, she is boiling fatback, ham hock, or streak o' lean in another pot of water. So she's got two pots going, because the way she sees it, you need to clean the beans first. Then you add them to the boiling fatback. The idea is that the cooking water is flavored even before the beans go in it; that way, they absorb maximum fatback flavor.

"These beans are simmered with a lid on so you keep all the fluid. But with green beans, Mama wanted the fluid out, so she simmered them without a lid."

1	pound white beans, rinsed and picked over
½	plus ½ gallon water
½	pound fatback or ham hock, cut into 4 strips
¼	cup butter
1	large onion, halved
1	garlic clove, peeled
½	teaspoon cracked red pepper
1	tablespoon salt
1	tablespoon black pepper

Boil the beans in ½ gallon water for 10 minutes. Set aside for 10 minutes. Drain and add the remaining ½ gallon water and bring to a boil. Add the fatback or ham hock and boil for 10 minutes. Heat the butter in a skillet over medium-high heat. Add the onion, garlic, cracked red pepper and sauté until the garlic starts to turn brown. Add to the stockpot with the beans and simmer on low heat, covered, for 1½ to 2 hours. Take your time, and then add the salt and pepper. The beans should be whole, tender, and tasty.

MAKES 6 TO 8 SERVINGS

BLACK-EYED PEA CAKES

Tom explains these cakes as the natural result of the South's abundance of black-eyed peas. "You are taking something you have a lot of, and something that stores well, and making the most of it."

2¼	cups black-eyed peas
½	green pepper, diced
¼	onion, diced
½	tablespoon minced garlic
2	teaspoons salt
½	tablespoon black pepper
½	tablespoon dried mustard
1	egg
	Flour for breading
	Egg wash for breading
½	cup breadcrumbs for breading
½	cup canola oil

Soak the black-eyed peas overnight and then drain off the excess water. Add fresh water to cover and boil the peas until tender. Drain the peas. Combine the pepper, onion, garlic, salt, pepper, mustard, and egg and mix in with the peas, stirring until incorporated. Using an ice cream scoop, scoop the mixture into round balls. Shape into patties about ½ inch thick. Dip the patties into the flour, then into the egg wash, and finally in the breadcrumbs. Refrigerate for at least 1 hour so the patties can firm. Pour the oil in a skillet over medium-high heat. Fry the patties for about 5 minutes on each side. Place them on a baking sheet and keep them warm in the oven at 200°F until ready to serve. Serve with a dollop of sour cream and sweet relish or chow-chow on the side.

MAKES 8 SERVINGS

DONNA'S BROCCOLI & RICE

A recipe handed down from former Loveless Cafe owner, Donna McCabe. Still a favorite.

1	small onion, chopped
1	tablespoon vegetable oil
1	(10-ounce) package chopped broccoli, thawed
1	(10-ounce) can cream of mushroom soup
1	cup shredded American cheese
1	teaspoon salt
1½	cups cooked rice

Sauté the onion in the oil in a large skillet over medium heat. Add the broccoli and cook for 5 minutes, stirring constantly. Add the soup and bring to a boil, stirring frequently; reduce the heat to medium low. Add the cheese, salt, and rice; mix well. Cook until heated through. Serve hot.

MAKES 4 TO 5 SERVINGS

BROCCOLI CHICKEN CASSEROLE

Children tend to like chicken but not broccoli," Tom observes. "This is a good way to get them to eat what's good for them."

1	*(12-ounce) box wild rice (instant or regular)*
1	*(10 ¾-ounce) can cream of mushroom soup*
1	*(10 ¾-ounce) can cream of chicken soup*
1	*cup Hellmann's mayonnaise*
4	*(5-ounce) skinless, boneless chicken breasts, cut up*
1	*(12-ounce) package frozen broccoli (may substitute artichoke hearts)*
1	*cup shredded Cheddar cheese (optional)*

Cook the wild rice according to the package's directions.

Preheat the oven to 350°F. Mix the rice, mushroom soup, chicken soup, mayonnaise, chicken, and broccoli together in a baking dish and bake for 30 minutes or until bubbly. Cheddar cheese can be sprinkled on the top if desired.

MAKES 4 TO 6 SERVINGS

SQUASH CASSEROLE

Squash is so plentiful in the summertime, that cooks are always looking for new ways to cook it. Tom says that squash casserole is his favorite way.

8	to 10 fresh yellow squash
1	medium onion, chopped
1½	cups water
¼	teaspoon salt
	Dash of pepper
1	cup shredded Velveeta cheese
1	cup cracker crumbs

Preheat the oven to 350°F. Rinse the squash; cut off the ends and slice into 1-inch pieces. Combine the squash, onion, and water in a saucepan. Sprinkle with the salt and pepper and cook over medium heat until the vegetables are tender, stirring frequently; drain. Spoon the cooked vegetables into a 2-quart casserole. Stir in the Velveeta cheese. Sprinkle the cracker crumbs over the top. Bake for 15 to 20 minutes or until bubbly.

MAKES 6 TO 8 SERVINGS

YELLOW SQUASH

Yellow squash is easy to grow," Tom notes. "You can't kill it. It survives summer drought. It blooms and it blooms again. It is always plentiful."

10	yellow squash
¼	pound (1 stick) butter
2	Vidalia onions, chopped
	Salt and black pepper

Wash and quarter the squash. Steam in a skillet or saucepan until al dente. Heat the butter in a saucepan over medium-high heat. Sauté the onions until translucent. Add the steamed squash. Season with the salt and pepper to taste.

MAKES 6 TO 8 SERVINGS

SOUTHERN GREENS

The darker the green, the more nutritious it is," Tom says, noting that one of the great things to do is to mix several greens together. "Collards, turnips, mustard, and kale are a wonderful blend of tastes. Alone, mustard greens can be pretty strong. But boiled with some of the milder greens and plenty of fatback, you've got something delicious."

Greens

2	quarts water plus more as needed
1	pound fatback, cut into ½-inch-thick slices
10	bunches (1 pound each) greens, stems picked and well rinsed
1	cup apple cider vinegar or mild red pepper sauce
½	cup salt

Vinegar pepper sauce

3	cups water
1	cup white vinegar
1	garlic clove, peeled
1	tablespoon sugar
1	tablespoon salt
4	Tabasco peppers

In a large stockpot bring the water and fatback to a boil over medium heat and cook for 10 minutes. Add the greens, vinegar or red pepper sauce, and salt. Boil the greens until tender, about 1½ hours, adding water as needed. As a saucy substitute you can use a half beer–half water mixture to cook the greens.

To make the vinegar pepper sauce, bring the water, vinegar, garlic, sugar, salt, and peppers to boil in a large stockpot and reduce in half. Drizzle the sauce over the greens with a spoon and serve.

MAKES 10 TO 12 SERVINGS

Note: The most important part of cooking greens is rinsing them. Rinse three times to insure no grit. Big batches make the whole process easier, and the greens freeze just fine.

GRILLED ZUCCHINI, ONIONS & RED PEPPERS

An easy from-the-garden recipe to use when you fire up the outdoor grill to make chicken or any other meat.

4	zucchini
2	red bell peppers
1	large sweet onion
¼	cup olive oil
¼	cup balsamic vinegar
1	garlic clove, chopped
⅛	cup chopped fresh basil
⅛	cup chopped fresh oregano
1	tablespoon kosher or sea salt
1	tablespoon coarse-ground black pepper

Trim the ends of the zucchini. Cut them in half lengthwise and then repeat until all the zucchini are quartered lengthwise. Trim, core, and stem the red peppers. Cut them into four equal parts from top down. Peel the onion and lay it on its side, and cut it into ¼ to ½-inch circles, being careful to keep the concentric layers in place. Place the zucchini, onions, and bell peppers in a shallow baking sheet. Combine the olive oil and balsamic vinegar and drizzle over the vegetables. Sprinkle the chopped garlic, basil, and oregano over the top. Add coarse-ground salt and cracked black pepper to taste. Place the vegetables on a hot grill with tongs. Cook on both sides for 2 to 3 minutes or until they are marked. When you turn the vegetables, brush on any remaining oil/vinegar mixture. Serve hot or cold.

MAKES 6 TO 8 SERVINGS

CREAM CORN

Cream corn is controversial. Traditional cooks insist that the way to get cream for the recipe is to cut the kernels off the cob in a way that about half of each kernel remains. Then you press or grate the remaining part of the kernels to retrieve enough "cream" for the recipe. Tom notes that this old-time technique works well if you are cooking a small amount, but for more than six people, you will likely need to add dairy cream.

6	ears sweet corn (we prefer the Silver Queen variety)
½	pound (2 sticks) butter
	Salt and pepper
¼	cup water
¼	cup cream

Carefully cut half of the kernels of corn off each cob. Scrape the milk out of the remaining kernels. Place the butter, the cut kernels, and the milk from the corn scraping into a skillet and cook over medium heat. Salt and pepper to taste. Add water and cream and cook until thickened, about 20 minutes.

MAKES 4 TO 6 SERVINGS

FRIED CORN

I call this skillet corn," Tom explains. "I cook it so it gets a nice brown crust; and I go one step further and add chopped onions. But onions do tend to offend some people, so this recipe excludes them."

6	ears Silver Queen or other white corn
½	cup bacon drippings
¼	plus ¼ cup (1 stick) butter
	Salt and pepper
2	cups water
1	cup milk

Over a large cast-iron skillet cut and scrape the corn off the cobs with the milky corn liquid. Turn the heat to high. Add the bacon drippings and 1/4 cup of the butter to the skillet. Add salt and pepper to taste. Cook for 3 minutes browning the corn before stirring. Stir in the milk and continue cooking until the milk is absorbed. Reduce the heat to medium and add the remaining ¼ cup butter. Cook until the butter is melted and mixed throughout.

MAKES 4 TO 6 SERVINGS

CORNBREAD DRESSING

Every southern home has cornbread," Tom observes. "White bread is something you have to bake in a loaf whereas corn bread you can cook and serve in a skillet. So in the old days when a recipe called for breadcrumbs, cornbread is generally what was on hand. At the Loveless, we make our stuffing out of cornbread and biscuits because that is what we always have."

1	10-inch, cast-iron skillet of Heavenly Cornbread (see page 39—can be made a day ahead)
7	or 8 small biscuits
1	large onion, chopped
2	celery stalks, finely chopped
3	eggs
	Salt and pepper
1	stick butter, melted
	Chicken broth for thinning

Butter a 9 x 13-inch pan and preheat the oven to 400°F. Crumble the cornbread and biscuits into a large mixing bowl. Add the onion, celery, eggs, salt and pepper to taste, and butter. Mix thoroughly and, while stirring, add enough chicken broth (about 2 cups) to thin the mixture so you can pour it. Pour the mixture into the prepared pan and bake for 30 minutes or until brown.

MAKES 6 TO 8 SERVINGS

LIB'S CHOW-CHOW

If you are serving black-eyed peas, you must have chow-chow," Tom says. "You can make it hot or mild; but it is essential."

2	pounds cabbage, chopped
12	onions, chopped
12	green bell peppers, chopped
12	red bell peppers, chopped
8	cups peeled and chopped green tomatoes
½	cup salt
5	cups sugar
4	tablespoons prepared mustard
1	tablespoon turmeric
1	tablespoon ground ginger
1	tablespoon mustard seed
3	tablespoons celery seed
2	tablespoons whole spices, pickling mix
8	to 12 cups vinegar

Combine the cabbage, onions, green and red bell peppers, tomatoes, and salt in a large bowl. Soak the mixture overnight and drain. In a large saucepan over medium heat combine the sugar, mustard, turmeric, ginger, mustard seed, celery seed, whole spices, and vinegar. Simmer this mixture for 20 minutes. Add the vegetables and simmer until hot and well seasoned. Pack the chow-chow into hot, sterilized half-pint jars, leaving ½ inch headspace. Cover with a ⅛-inch layer of paraffin; seal with 2-piece lids. Heat the jars in a boiling water bath for 10 minutes to seal the lids.

MAKES 10 TO 12 JARS

GREEN TOMATO CHOW-CHOW

Green tomatoes found their way into chow-chow as a way of making the most of abundant garden produce.

2½	pounds (about 8) green tomatoes, peeled and chopped
2	onions, chopped or sliced
2	tablespoons salt
¾	cup sugar
½	tablespoon whole spices, pickling mix
2	cups vinegar

Combine the tomatoes, onions, and salt in a large bowl. Soak the mixture overnight and drain. In a large saucepan over medium heat combine the sugar, spices, and vinegar. Simmer this mixture for 20 minutes. Add the tomatoes and onions and simmer until hot and well seasoned. Pack the chow-chow into hot, sterilized half-pint jars, leaving ½ inch headspace. Cover with a ⅛-inch layer of paraffin; seal with 2-piece lids. Heat the jars in a boiling water bath for 10 minutes to seal the lids.

MAKES 4 TO 6 JARS

Note: If desired you may also add 1 teaspoon ginger, 2 teaspoons celery seed, and 2 teaspoons turmeric.

SWEET POTATO CASSEROLE

Tom declares: "Marshmallows are essential. Full size or minis are fine, and while the big ones came first, minis work better." He further adds that sweet potato casserole is one of the absolute essentials at a turkey dinner.

Potatoes

3	cups peeled and quartered sweet potatoes (about 4 large)
½	cup sugar
½	cup (1 stick) butter
2	eggs, beaten
1	teaspoon vanilla extract
⅓	cup milk

Topping

⅓	cup butter, melted
1	cup light brown sugar
½	cup all-purpose flour
1	cup chopped pecans

Boil and mash the potatoes. Mix in the sugar, butter, eggs, vanilla, and milk. Pour into a 13 x 9-inch baking dish. Preheat the oven to 350°F.

For the topping, mix the melted butter with the brown sugar, flour, and pecans. Sprinkle the mix on top of the potatoes. Bake for 25 minutes.

MAKES 10 TO 12 SERVINGS

CORN & POTATO GRATIN

Y ou've got corn and you've got potatoes," Tom explains. "So you make the best of them by creating an au gratin. This is a traditional variation."

1⅓	diced leeks, white part only
2	teaspoons olive oil
3⅓	cups peeled and diced Yukon gold potatoes
2	cups roasted sweet corn, cut from the cob
1⅓	cups grated Gruyere or Manchego cheese*
2½	cups heavy cream
2	teaspoons salt
2	teaspoons chipotle powder
⅔	cup rinsed and chopped Italian parsley

Sauté the leeks in the olive oil until translucent. Place the leeks, potatoes, corn, cheese, cream, salt, chipotle powder, and parsley into a bowl and toss until combined. Place in a large baking dish. Bake at 350°F, covered with parchment paper and foil, until bubbly and the potatoes are tender. Remove the parchment and foil and continue to bake until a good crust forms on top.

MAKES 8 SERVINGS

*Note: You can use your favorite cheese, such as Cheddar or American, instead.

BLACK-EYED PEAS

The most popular of the field peas store well and are available year-round. The same is true of cornmeal, which is why so many traditional meals include corn bread, black-eyed peas, and chow-chow. None of these elements is seasonal.

2	*cups dried black-eyed peas*
4	*cups water*
8	*ounces fatback*
1¾	*teaspoons salt*
1¾	*teaspoons pepper*
2	*teaspoons red pepper flakes*
1	*tablespoon minced garlic*
2	*small white onions, halved*

Rinse and soak the peas until tender, about 8 hours. Drain. Cover the peas with water and boil for 3 to 5 minutes. Drain, rinse, and set aside. Add the water and fatback to the pot and boil for 10 minutes. Add the peas, salt, pepper, red pepper, garlic, and onions and cook until tender, about 20 minutes.

MAKES 8 SERVINGS

Desserts

Apple Turnovers

Apple Cake

Chocolate Soufflé

Chocolate Cake with Ganache Frosting

Carrot Cake with Cream Cheese Frosting

Hummingbird Cake

Lemon Bundt Cake

Blackberry Cobbler

Strawberry-Rhubarb Cobbler

Peach Cobbler

Lazy Day Cobbler

Pie Dough

Coconut Cream Pie

Pecan Pie

Apple Pie

Blueberry Pie

Peanut Butter Pie

Peach Pie

Fudge Pie

Lemon Icebox Pie

Sweet Potato Pie

Banana Pudding

Rice Pudding

Bread Pudding

Caramel Sauce

Orange Blossom Special

Linzer Cookies

Brownies

Graham Cracker Squares

Chess Squares

Turtle Squares

Snickerdoodles

Jam Bars

Chocolate Biscuit Pudding

Caramel Filling

Caramel Pie

Applesauce Pie

Peach Custard Pie

Red Velvet Cake

Chocolate Zucchini Cake

Oatmeal Cookies

APPLE TURNOVERS

Alisa Huntsman likes this recipe for turnovers because it doesn't require a lot of cooking skill. As she puts it: "It's a little of this, a little of that, a few apples in a bowl, and there it is."

1	sheet frozen puff pastry, thawed
1½	Granny Smith apples, peeled, cored, and thinly sliced
¼	cup firmly packed brown sugar
1	tablespoon unbleached all-purpose flour
1	teaspoon ground cinnamon
½	teaspoon ground nutmeg
¼	teaspoon cloves
1	egg
1	tablespoon water
	Sugar for sprinkling

Preheat the oven to 400°F. Cut the pastry into 6 equal squares—3 across the long side, 2 down the short side. Place the cut dough on a large baking sheet and keep in the refrigerator until ready to fill. Toss the apples, brown sugar, flour, cinnamon, nutmeg, and cloves together in a bowl. Allow to sit for 10 to 15 minutes so that the apples can juice a little. Remove the dough from the refrigerator and portion out the apples onto the dough squares. Place the apples so that they are in the center of one-half of each square on the diagonal. Make an egg wash by beating the egg and water together. Brush the sides lightly with the egg wash. Fold the dough over the apples and line up the corners to create triangles. Press to seal. Brush the tops with the egg wash and sprinkle with the sugar. Bake for 15 to 20 minutes or until evenly golden.

MAKES 6 SERVINGS

APPLE CAKE

Here is a recipe that dates back to Alisa's high school cooking class, where she and her teacher, Mrs. Saslow, knew that she was destined to go to the Culinary Institute of America and to cook for a living. "I was the teacher's pet, so she gave me the challenges," Alisa recalls. "Apple cake was one of them."

2	cups sugar
1½	cups canola oil
4	large eggs
3	cups unbleached all-purpose flour
1	teaspoon ground cinnamon
½	teaspoon ground nutmeg
¼	teaspoon ground cloves
1	teaspoon baking soda
3	Granny Smith apples, peeled, cored, and roughly chopped
½	cup chopped walnuts or pecans

Preheat the oven to 350°F. Combine the sugar, oil, and eggs in a bowl and whisk together. Mix together the flour, cinnamon, nutmeg, cloves, and baking soda and sift it over the sugar mixture. Fold in gently. Gently fold the apples and nuts into the batter. Pour into a Bundt, tube, or other large decorative pan that has been greased and floured. Bake for 50 minutes to 1 hour or until a toothpick inserted in the cake comes out clean. Cool in the pan for 10 minutes and then invert onto a cooling rack to finish cooling. When completely cooled, cake can be sliced and served with Caramel Sauce (see page 186).

MAKES 12 TO 16 SERVINGS

CHOCOLATE SOUFFLÉ

A classic dessert that is at once unspeakably rich and featherlight. This is one dish that cannot be made in advance. You want to serve it warm, not long out of the oven.

2	tablespoons butter
2	tablespoons all-purpose flour
1½	(1-ounce) chocolate squares
2	tablespoons hot water
¾	cup milk
2	egg yolks, beaten
2	egg whites
	Whipped cream

Preheat the oven to 300°F to 325°F. Melt the butter in a saucepan over medium-low heat. Add the flour, stirring until well blended. Dissolve the chocolate in the hot water in a small bowl; add to the butter mixture. Stir in the milk. Remove from the heat. Add the egg yolks; mix well. Let stand until cool. Beat the egg whites until stiff peaks form; fold into the chocolate mixture. Pour into a buttered 9 x 13-inch baking dish. Bake for 20 minutes. Top each serving with a dollop of whipped cream.

MAKES 6 TO 8 SERVINGS

CHOCOLATE CAKE WITH GANACHE FROSTING

Alisa, an admitted chocoholic, calls this recipe foolproof. "You cannot kill this cake!" she exults, noting that the recipe is especially useful because it can be made into cupcakes or sheet cakes, and it can be frosted or served with whipped cream and strawberries. "I made this for my best friend's wedding," she says.

Cake

2	cups unbleached all-purpose flour
2	cups sugar
½	cup cocoa powder
2	teaspoons baking soda
1	teaspoon baking powder
1	teaspoon salt
1	cup milk
1	cup freshly brewed coffee at room temperature
1	cup canola oil
2	large eggs
2	teaspoons vanilla extract

Ganache

16	ounces semisweet or bittersweet chocolate
1	cup sour cream at room temperature
2	tablespoons light corn syrup

For the cake, preheat the oven to 350°F. Combine the flour, sugar, cocoa powder, baking soda, baking powder, and salt and sift into a large bowl. Stir to incorporate. Using a whisk, mix the milk, coffee, and oil into the dry ingredients. Whisk the egg and vanilla into the batter. Pour into two 9-inch cake pans that have been greased and floured. Bake for about 35 minutes or until a toothpick comes out clean. Cool in the pans. When completely cooled, briefly heat the bottom of the pans on the stovetop and turn out the cake layers. Place the layers in the refrigerator to chill all the way through. This will make slicing them easier.

For the ganache, melt the chocolate over barely simmering water. When melted, remove from the heat and stir in the sour cream and corn syrup.

Slice each cake layer in half, making four layers. Place one layer on a serving dish or cardboard circle and top with ½ cup of the ganache. Spread it evenly and top with another layer. Repeat until all four layers are stacked. Put the remaining ganache on the top of the cake, spreading it over the top and sides. Chill the cake before serving to set the frosting. The cake will taste best at room temperature. To cut, dip a sharp knife in hot water and the knife will glide through the cake. Wipe it off and dip it again for each cut you make.

MAKES 12 TO 16 SERVINGS

Note: Use high quality chocolate such as Ghirardelli, Lindt, Valhrona, Guittard or Callebaut. Do not use "baking" chocolate or "German chocolate" found in the baking aisle of the supermarket.

CARROT CAKE WITH CREAM CHEESE FROSTING

Truly the world's best carrot cake recipe!" Alisa declares, noting that back in San Francisco she used to make it with fresh pineapple, but that here in Tennessee the PH in the fresh fruit caused the cake to fall. Hence the use of canned pineapple in the recipe.

Cake

2	cups unbleached all-purpose flour
2	cups granulated sugar
½	teaspoon salt
2	teaspoons baking soda
2	teaspoons ground cinnamon
1	cup chopped walnuts
2	cups shredded carrots
½	cup drained and crushed pineapple
1	cup shredded coconut
1	cup canola oil
3	large eggs
1	teaspoon vanilla extract

Cream cheese frosting

8	ounces softened cream cheese
6	tablespoons softened butter
1	teaspoon vanilla extract
3	cups sifted confectioners' sugar
	Chopped walnuts (optional)

To make the cake, preheat the oven to 350°F. Sift together the flour, sugar, salt, baking soda, and cinnamon into a bowl and stir together. Combine the walnuts, carrots, pineapple, and coconut in a bowl. Add the oil, eggs, and vanilla to the dry ingredients and stir to combine. Add the carrot mix and blend together. Pour into three 9-inch cake pans that have been greased and floured. Bake for 25 to 35 minutes or until a toothpick comes out clean. Refrigerate in the pans. To remove from the pans, briefly heat the bottom of the pans on the stove and flip out onto a piece of parchment.

To make the frosting, combine the cream cheese, butter, vanilla, and confectioners' sugar in a mixing bowl and cream together. Spread ⅓ cup between the layers and the remaining frosting over the top and sides. To garnish, use chopped walnuts on the sides of the cake.

MAKES 12 TO 16 SERVINGS

HUMMINGBIRD CAKE

Hummingbird cake is popular throughout the South and often found in cookbooks published by Junior Leagues and church groups.

3	cups unbleached all-purpose flour
2	cups granulated sugar
1	teaspoon salt
1	teaspoon baking soda
1	teaspoon ground cinnamon
3	large eggs
1	cup canola oil
1	teaspoon vanilla extract
1	cup crushed pineapple (do not drain)
1	cup chopped pecans plus more for topping
2	cups mashed bananas

Preheat the oven to 350°F. Combine the flour, sugar, salt, baking soda, and cinnamon and sift into a bowl. Stir together. Add the eggs, oil, and vanilla to the dry ingredients and mix to moisten. Add the pineapple, pecans, and bananas to the batter and mix in. Pour into three 9-inch cake pans that have been floured and greased. Bake for 25 to 35 minutes or until a toothpick comes out clean. Refrigerate in the pans. To remove from the pans, briefly heat the bottom of the pans on the stove and flip out onto a piece of parchment. Garnish with chopped pecans.

MAKES 3 (9-INCH) CAKES

Alisa Huntsman

Alisa Huntsman did not graduate from the Culinary Institute of America in Hyde Park, New York, in 1983 intending to become a pastry chef at a cafe in Nashville, Tennessee. Her first job was in the kitchen of the Vista Hotel in the World Trade Center in lower Manhattan; she then worked in restaurants in DC and San Francisco. It was only after some experience as a line cook that she realized her real calling was not making sandwiches and salads or working on the flat top grill, but baking.

There didn't used to be a pastry chef at the Loveless Cafe because there were no pastries on the menu. In fact, there was no dessert at all. When the place was reconfigured in 2004, one of the biggest changes was a new and separate dinner menu. In the past, the restaurant was open for dinner, but the menu was the same as it was for breakfast and for lunch: basically, fried chicken and ham. Along with new entrées for dinner, a roster of desserts was essential. Alisa and her husband, wanting to move away from the overwrought culinary ferment of the Bay Area, were ready to take the plunge and move into the heartland. While she confesses that she does not find enough classical music on the radio, it is clear she has found her calling as a baker in the new Loveless Cafe.

Banana pudding, a Dixie kitchen classic, shows how devoted to the task she is. "I decided that if I was going to do it, I was going to do it right," she says. "I wasn't satisfied with ordinary vanilla wafers. Those things that come in the box are cute . . . if you're four years old. But they taste too artificial for me." Unable to find a recipe for the little round cookies that are an absolutely essential ingredient in traditional banana pudding, Alisa did come up with a recipe for a French ladyfinger-type cookie called a *boudoir*. She actually left out the vanilla and made her own wafers with a basic formula of eggs, sugar, and flour. Combined with custard that is fresh rather than instant, as well as sliced ripe bananas, the result is a pudding that is true to the southern cook's canon, and yet transcendent.

LEMON BUNDT CAKE

This cake is one of the many uses of the basic muffin recipe. This is virtually the same, but here put into a different-shaped pan.

¼	pound (1 stick) unsalted butter, melted and cooled
1¼	cups granulated sugar
¼	teaspoon salt
2	large eggs at room temperature
1½	teaspoons lemon extract or zest of 2 lemons
2⅓	cups unbleached all-purpose flour
2	teaspoons baking powder
⅔	cup buttermilk
	Blackberry preserves

Glaze

3	cups confectioners' sugar
2	tablespoons lemon juice

For the cake, whisk the butter, sugar, salt, eggs, and lemon extract together in a bowl. Sift the flour and baking powder into the egg mixture and gently fold a few times. Add the buttermilk to the mix and finish folding together. Preheat the oven to 350°F. Prepare a Bundt pan by greasing and flouring it. Spoon half the batter into the mold. Top with a thin ring of blackberry preserves (any berry flavor will work) and top with the remaining batter. Be careful not to allow the preserves to touch the sides of the pan or the cake will stick badly. Bake for about 1 hour or until a toothpick comes out clean. Allow to cool for 10 minutes and then invert the cake onto a rack. Allow to cool for 30 minutes.

For the glaze, sift the confectioners' sugar into a bowl. Add the lemon juice and enough water to make a slightly thick glaze. Pour the mixture over the cake.

MAKES 18 TO 20 SERVINGS

BLACKBERRY COBBLER

Cobbler is hugely popular throughout the South, crowned with pie dough, biscuit topping, or sweetened crumbs. It is always served warm, and at the Loveless, ice cream is optional.

Dough

2	cups unbleached all-purpose flour
¼	cup firmly packed brown sugar
½	teaspoon salt
2	teaspoons baking powder
¼	pound (1 stick) cold unsalted butter, cut into cubes
8	ounces heavy cream

Filling

1	pound frozen unsweetened blackberries, thawed, with juice
½	cup granulated sugar plus more for sprinkling
1	tablespoon rosewater
2	tablespoons cornstarch
	Melted butter

For the dough, combine the flour, sugar, salt, and baking powder in a bowl. Cut in the butter until it resembles meal or small crumbs. Add the cream to the mix to form a soft dough. Place in the refrigerator until the filling is ready.

For the filling, combine the blackberries, sugar, rosewater, and cornstarch and pour into a 9-inch cake pan. Roll the crust ¼ to ½-inch thick and cut it to fit the top of the dish. Preheat the oven to 375°F.

To assemble, place the dough over the filling. Brush it with the melted butter and sprinkle with the remaining granulated sugar. Bake on a metal baking tray for 30 to 40 minutes or until the filling boils around the edges and the topping is golden brown.

MAKES 8 TO 10 SERVINGS

STRAWBERRY-RHUBARB COBBLER

Rhubarb is an old southern thing," Tom says, "But I believe that cooking it is a dying art. I don't really know why. Perhaps it is because the name just isn't that attractive. For some reason people treat rhubarb with contempt. That's too bad, because it mixes so well with other fruits in pies and cobblers."

Dough			Filling		
2	cups unbleached all-purpose flour		8	ounces frozen unsweetened strawberries, thawed, with juice	
¼	cup firmly packed brown sugar		8	ounces frozen rhubarb, thawed with juice	
½	teaspoon salt		½	cup firmly packed brown sugar	
2	teaspoons baking powder		¾	teaspoon ground cinnamon	
¼	pound (1 stick) cold, unsalted butter, cut into cubes		½	teaspoon ground nutmeg	
8	ounces heavy cream		½	teaspoon ground ginger	
			1	tablespoon cornstarch	
			Melted butter		
			Granulated sugar		

For the dough, combine the flour, sugar, salt, and baking powder in a bowl. Cut in the butter until it resembles meal or small crumbs. Add the cream to the mix to form a soft dough. Place in the refrigerator until the filling is ready.

For the filling, combine the fruit with the brown sugar, cinnamon, nutmeg, ginger, and cornstarch. Pour into a 9-inch cake pan. Roll the crust ¼ to ½-inch thick and cut it to fit the top of the dish. (If using fresh fruit, allow the juices to accumulate before topping the dish and baking it.) Preheat the oven to 375°F.

To assemble, place the dough over the filling. Brush it with the melted butter and sprinkle with the granulated sugar. Bake on a metal baking tray for 30 to 40 minutes, or until the filling boils around the edges and the topping is golden brown.

MAKES 8 TO 10 SERVINGS

Note: You can substitute 1½ cups fresh berries for the frozen.

PEACH COBBLER

Southern peaches are softer and sweeter," Tom explains. "That is why the tradition of peach cooking is so strong. With such a short shelf life, it is something that must be used; and cobbler is a great way to do it. That is why peach preserves are so popular, too."

Dough		**Filling**	
2	cups unbleached all-purpose flour	1	pound frozen sliced peaches, thawed, with juice
¼	cup firmly packed brown sugar	½	cup firmly packed brown sugar
½	teaspoon salt	¾	teaspoon ground cinnamon
2	teaspoons baking powder	¾	teaspoon pumpkin pie spice
¼	pound (1 stick) cold, unsalted butter, cut into cubes	½	teaspoon ground ginger
8	ounces heavy cream	1	tablespoon cornstarch
			Melted butter
			Granulated sugar

For the dough, combine the flour, sugar, salt, and baking powder in a bowl. Cut in the butter until it resembles meal or small crumbs. Add the cream to the mix to form a soft dough. Place in the refrigerator until the filling is ready.

For the filling, combine the fruit with the brown sugar, cinnamon, pumpkin pie spice, ginger, and cornstarch. (If using fresh fruit, allow the juices to accumulate before topping the dish and baking it.) Pour into a 9-inch cake pan. Roll the crust ¼ to ½-inch thick and cut it to fit the top of the dish. Preheat the oven to 375°F.

To assemble, place the dough over the filling. Brush it with the melted butter and sprinkle with the granulated sugar. Bake on a metal baking tray for 30 to 40 minutes, or until the filling boils around the edges and the topping is golden brown.

MAKES 8 TO 10 SERVINGS

Note: You can substitute 1½ cups fresh berries for the frozen.

LAZY DAY COBBLER

Tom's advice for making cobbler: "When there is nothing at all available from the garden, use a can!"

½	cup (1 stick) butter
1	plus ½ cup sugar
1	cup all-purpose flour
¾	cup milk
1½	teaspoons baking powder
¼	teaspoon salt
1	(16-ounce) can pitted unsweetened cherries (not drained)

Preheat the oven to 350°F. Place the butter in a deep-dish pan and melt it in the oven. Beat together the 1 cup sugar, flour, milk, baking powder, and salt into a smooth batter and pour it over the butter. Do not stir. Empty the cherries (not drained) over the batter and sprinkle with the remaining ½ cup sugar. Bake for 30 to 45 minutes. The batter will rise to the top.

MAKES 8 SERVINGS

Note: You can substitute peaches, blackberries, or pineapple for the cherries.

PIE DOUGH

Making your own pie dough is the real deal," Tom declares. "While there are good imitations on the market, good homemade dough is the secret to pie."

6   cups unbleached all-purpose flour

1   tablespoon salt

1   pound plus 4 tablespoons cold, unsalted butter, cut into cubes

9   tablespoons cold water

3   tablespoons white vinegar

Place the flour, salt, and butter in a mixer bowl with a flat beater and cut to the size of small peas. Add the water and vinegar and mix until the dough is incorporated. Divide into six equal pieces and shape into disks. Chill the dough for 2 hours to relax the proteins and make it easier to roll out.

To roll out the dough, allow it to soften so that it is pliable and use plenty of flour to prevent it from sticking. Turn the dough continually to maintain a round shape. Using a soft brush, remove the excess flour before placing the crust in a pie pan. Make sure that the dough hangs over the side of the pan by 1 inch. Roll the edges under and pinch them upwards to form a raised crust. Flute the edges using your fingers. To use the crust, be sure to chill it for at least 30 minutes before baking. This will help retain the round shape and prevent shrinkage. Preheat the oven to 375°F.

To bake, line the pie shell with large coffee filters and fill the shell with weights. (We use ordinary dried beans; they are cheap, easy to find, and reusable.) Bake for 15 to 20 minutes, or until the edges barely begin to color. Remove from the oven and cool. Scoop out the beans and discard the filter. Fill and bake according to directions.

MAKES ENOUGH DOUGH FOR 6 (9-INCH) PIE CRUSTS

Note: The dough can be rolled out, shaped into crusts, and the shells not needed immediately can be frozen for future use, or just freeze the dough patties for later use.

COCONUT CREAM PIE

I threw this together the first week I was at the Loveless, and it became probably the most popular pie we have," Alisa says.

1	*(10-inch) baked pie shell*

Filling

1½	*cups toasted coconut shreds*
2	*cups half-and-half*
½	*cup sugar*
3	*large eggs*
1	*teaspoon vanilla extract*

Topping

2	*cups heavy cream*
2	*tablespoons sugar*
1	*teaspoon vanilla extract*

White chocolate shavings or toasted coconut for garnish

Preheat the oven to 375°F. Place the coconut shreds in the pie shell. Place the pie shell on a baking pan that is lined with foil and coated with cooking spray. Whisk together the half-and-half, sugar, eggs, and vanilla and pour the mixture over the coconut. Bake for about 35 minutes or until golden on top, puffy around the edges, and firm in the center. Cool completely before topping.

For the topping, combine the cream, sugar, and vanilla and whip until stiff peaks form. Spread the topping evenly over the pie. Garnish with white chocolate shavings or toasted coconut.

MAKES 8 SERVINGS

PECAN PIE

Alisa refers to pecan pie as being based on the translucent custard concept. She notes that chocolate pecan pie is every bit as popular as this basic one.

1	(10-inch) baked pie shell
1½	cups pecans (halves or pieces)
3	large eggs
1	cup light corn syrup
½	cup firmly packed brown sugar
1	teaspoon vanilla extract
¼	teaspoon ground cinnamon
4	tablespoons unsalted butter, melted

Preheat the oven to 375°F. Place the pecans in the pie shell and place the shell on a prepared baking sheet. Whisk together the eggs, corn syrup, brown sugar, vanilla, and cinnamon. Whisk the melted butter into the egg mix. Pour the mixture over the pecans. Bake for 35 to 40 minutes, or until puffed and firm in the center.

MAKES 8 SERVINGS

APPLE PIE

Firm, tart apples are essential for good apple pie. If Granny Smiths are not available, Pippins will work well, too.

2	rounds of Pie Dough (see page 172)

Filling

4	to 6 peeled, cored, and sliced Granny Smith apples (about 6 cups)
¾	cup firmly packed brown sugar
2	tablespoons cornstarch
2	teaspoons ground cinnamon
1	teaspoon ground nutmeg
¼	teaspoon cloves
¼	teaspoon cardamom
½	teaspoon ground ginger
1	tablespoon heavy cream
1	large egg
1	tablespoon water
	Cinnamon-sugar

Roll out one piece of dough, making sure it is large enough to hang over a 9-inch pan by 1 inch on all sides. Place the dough in the refrigerator. Roll out the other piece of dough slightly smaller. Place it on a baking sheet lined with paper and place in the refrigerator until the filling is prepared.

To make the filling, toss together the apples, brown sugar, cornstarch, cinnamon, nutmeg, cloves, cardamom, ginger, and cream. Allow the apples to juice for 30 minutes. Remove the crusts from the refrigerator and allow them to soften. Whisk together the egg and water to make an egg wash. Brush the egg wash on the edge of the bottom crust. Preheat the oven to 375°F. Pour in the filling. Cut slits or a center hole in the top crust and place it over the filling. Press the edges to seal, roll the top crust under the bottom crust, and pinch and crimp it. Brush the egg wash over the top and sprinkle with cinnamon-sugar to taste. Bake for about 1 hour, or until the juices are boiling in the center of the pie. If the crust is getting too dark, drape a piece of parchment paper over the top of the pie.

MAKES 8 SERVINGS

BLUEBERRY PIE

J esse said his friends told him that this is one of the best blueberry pies they ever had," Alisa relates, pointing out that this recipe works equally well with fresh or frozen blueberries.

1	(9-inch) unbaked pie shell (see page 172; use scraps of dough for decorating pie, or use commercial unbaked crust)

Filling

1¼	pounds frozen blueberries (about 4 cups), thawed
½	cup sugar
	Zest and juice of 1 lemon
2	teaspoons rosewater
¾	teaspoon ground ginger
2	tablespoons cornstarch

Combine the berries, sugar, lemon zest and juice, rosewater, ginger, and cornstarch and mix well. Allow to sit and accumulate juices for a while. Place the pie shell on a prepared pan. Pour the filling into the pie shell and use a remaining piece of dough to make a lattice top or small cutout shapes such as hearts or dots. Place the pieces on top of the filling, and bake at 375°F until the juices boil in the center of the pie. Allow the pie to cool and sit several hours before cutting.

MAKES 8 SERVINGS

Note: You can substitute fresh blueberries for the frozen. If using fresh, crush 1 cup of the berries to make juice.

PEANUT BUTTER PIE

I had never eaten peanut butter pie when I first made this," Alisa confesses. I am generally not a big fan of peanut butter as a dessert. I prefer it in a peanut butter and jelly sandwich, or perhaps in a peanut butter cookie. But I tasted as I developed the recipe, and now people tell me that they love it. It's probably our most popular non-fruit pie."

Filling

¾	cup light corn syrup
½	cup firmly packed brown sugar
½	cup smooth peanut butter
3	large eggs
1	teaspoon vanilla extract
⅓	cup half-and-half
1	baked (9-inch) pie shell (see page 172)

Topping

2	cups heavy cream
2	tablespoons granulated sugar
1	teaspoon vanilla extract

White chocolate shavings or toasted coconut for garnish

Preheat the oven to 375°F. Whisk together the corn syrup, brown sugar, peanut butter, eggs, vanilla, and half-and-half until smooth. Pour into the pie shell and bake for 30 minutes or until puffy around the edges and almost firm in the center. Cool completely and top with whipped cream.

For the topping, combine the cream, sugar, and vanilla and whip until stiff. Spread evenly over the pie. Garnish with white chocolate shavings or toasted coconut.

MAKES 8 SERVINGS

PEACH PIE

Cherry and apple pie may be the big ones in most of America, but in the South, and especially at the Loveless, peach pie rules.

Filling

1	pound frozen sliced peaches, thawed, with juice
½	cup firmly packed brown sugar
¾	teaspoon ground cinnamon
¾	teaspoon pumpkin pie spice
½	teaspoon ground ginger
1	tablespoon cornstarch
1	(9-inch) unbaked pie shell (see page 172; use scraps of dough for decorating pie, or use commercial unbaked crust)

For the filling, combine the peaches with the brown sugar, cinnamon, pumpkin spice, ginger, and cornstarch. Allow the mixture to sit and accumulate juices for a while.

Preheat the oven to 375°F. Place the pie shell on a prepared pan. Pour the filling into the pie shell and use any remaining pieces of dough to make a lattice top or small cutout shapes such as hearts or dots. Place the pieces of dough on top of the filling and bake for 45 minutes, or until juices boil in the center of the pie. Allow to cool and sit several hours before cutting.

MAKES 8 SERVINGS

Note: You can substitute fresh peaches for the frozen.

FUDGE PIE

Alisa advises that there is no need to buy expensive, fancy chocolate for fudge pie filling. Supermarket chocolate works fine.

1   (9-inch) baked pie shell (see page 172)

Filling

1¼   cups corn syrup

⅔   cup firmly packed brown sugar

4   large eggs

1¼   teaspoons vanilla extract

2½   ounces unsweetened chocolate, melted

6   tablespoons half-and-half

Topping

2   cups heavy cream

2   tablespoons sugar

1   teaspoon vanilla extract

         Chocolate curls (optional)

Preheat the oven to 375°F. Place the pie shell on a prepared baking sheet. Whisk together the corn syrup, brown sugar, eggs, and vanilla in a bowl. Combine the chocolate and the half-and-half. Pour the chocolate mixture into the egg mixture and whisk together. Pour the filling into the pie shell and bake until puffy and almost firm in the center, 20 to 30 minutes.

For the topping, combine the cream, sugar, and vanilla and whip until stiff. When the pie has cooled completely, spread the whipped cream evenly over the pie. Decorate with chocolate curls, if desired.

MAKES 8 SERVINGS

LEMON ICEBOX PIE

The old south version of Key Lime pie is especially popular in Tennessee. It's a refreshing dessert that is especially welcome in the summer, or after a hot barbecue meal that leaves the tongue with a pepper glow that needs quenching.

1	(15-ounce) can sweetened condensed milk
½	cup lemon juice
1	teaspoon grated lemon rind
2	egg yolks, beaten
1	(9-inch) graham cracker pie shell
2	egg whites
3	tablespoons sugar

Preheat the oven to 350°F. Combine the condensed milk, lemon juice, lemon rind, and egg yolks in a mixing bowl; mix well. Pour into the graham cracker pie shell. Beat the egg whites in a small mixing bowl until soft peaks form. Gradually add the sugar, beating until stiff peaks form. Spread over the filling, sealing to the edge. Bake until the meringue is light brown. Chill, covered, until serving time. Serve cold.

MAKES 6 SERVINGS

SWEET POTATO PIE

Alisa says, "For me, making sweet potato pie was a learning experience. Being from the north, it was not something I ever knew. In my family in New Milford, New Jersey, we ate our sweet potatoes baked, with butter. I especially like this recipe because of the maple syrup."

3	sweet potatoes, baked and skinned
1½	tablespoons unsalted butter, melted
2	tablespoons pure maple syrup
¼	cup packed dark brown sugar
½	teaspoon ground cinnamon
¼	teaspoon ground nutmeg
2	eggs
6	tablespoons heavy cream
1	(9-inch) prebaked pie shell (see page 172)

Preheat the oven to 350°F. In a bowl mash together the potatoes, butter, syrup, and sugar. Whisk in the cinnamon, nutmeg, and eggs. Carefully stir in the cream. Pour the potato mixture into the pie shell and bake for about 25 minutes or until the sides begin to puff up and the center is not quite set. (The temperature of the potatoes will affect the baking time. If using cold leftover potatoes, the pie will need longer baking time.) Remove from the oven and cool before serving.

MAKES 6 TO 8 SERVINGS

BANANA PUDDING

I used to have an aversion to banana pudding," Alisa laughs. "To me, it had always seemed like chain restaurant food: open a can of pudding and dump it into a bowl with banana slices and cookies. You see this on dessert buffets all around the country, and it's not pretty. When they told me they needed a banana pudding recipe, I said, no way I am using a can!" The result is a recipe for what we consider the best banana pudding there is.

Vanilla cream

½	cup cornstarch
1	quart whole milk
12	egg yolks
¼	vanilla bean, split and seeds scraped out
1¼	cups sugar

No nilla wafers

1	cup plus 2 tablespoons sugar
4	eggs
2⅓	cups unbleached all-purpose flour
1	to 2 cups sweetened whipped cream
4	to 6 bananas

For the vanilla cream, place the cornstarch in a bowl. Add enough of the milk to completely dissolve it. Add the egg yolks to the cornstarch and whisk together. Place the vanilla bean and sugar in a heavy-bottomed, stainless steel pot. Add the remaining milk and bring it to a boil. When the milk is boiling, reduce the heat slightly to prevent it from boiling over the sides of the pot. With a small ladle, whisk a small amount of the milk into the egg yolk mix. Repeat this step until one-third of the milk is mixed into the eggs. Whisk this mixture into the remaining boiling milk and return it to a boil while you continue to whisk it. The mix will thicken quickly. Continue whisking for 1 minute. Remove from the heat and pour the cream into a heat-proof dish. Press plastic wrap onto the surface and place in the refrigerator to cool.

For the wafers, place 1 cup of the sugar and eggs in a stainless steel bowl and whisk together. Place the bowl over simmering water and whisk until the sugar dissolves and the eggs are warmer than your body temperature. Immediately pour into the bowl of a stand mixer, and whip on high speed until the mixture forms mounds when you lift the beater out. Sift the flour over the eggs in several batches, folding it in gently. Preheat the oven to 375°F. Using a piping bag with a straight tip, pipe the batter out into quarter-size cookies. Sprinkle liberally with the remaining 2 tablespoons sugar and bake for 10 to 12 minutes or until completely golden to light brown.

To assemble, spread a small amount of the Vanilla Cream in a decorative trifle dish. Top with a layer of sliced fresh bananas and then a layer of cookies. Spread enough vanilla cream over this to create a smooth and level surface. Repeat these steps to fill the dish, ending with a layer of the cream. Wrap well and allow the pudding to sit 6 to 8 hours or overnight in the refrigerator. Before serving, decorate with the whipped cream, cookies, and banana slices.

MAKES 12 SERVINGS

RICE PUDDING

I used to make rice pudding in my bakery," Alisa recalls. "I cooked it on the stovetop, then baked it in the oven. One day, a woman who was a devoted rice pudding fan told me that it seemed a little dry. I did it on the stovetop but didn't then bake it. The result was a really creamy pudding." She says that basmati rice is best because it doesn't get mushy, and it gives the most flavor when it is cooked soft, as rice for rice pudding ought to be.

5	*cups whole milk*
2	*cinnamon sticks*
¼	*vanilla bean, split and scraped*
½	*cup basmati rice*
⅔	*cup sugar*
6	*egg yolks*
	Cinnamon-sugar for topping
	Whipped cream for topping

Combine the milk, cinnamon sticks, and vanilla bean in a heavy-bottom pot. Bring to a boil. Turn off the heat and allow the mix to steep 30 minutes. Return the milk to medium heat. Add the rice and simmer until the rice is tender, about 20 minutes. Whisk together the sugar and egg yolks. Add one-third of the hot rice-milk mix and whisk it in. Pour this mixture into the remaining hot milk-rice and whisk to combine. Continue whisking over low heat until the mixture thickens. Do not boil the mix; allow it to thicken to a soft pudding consistency and then remove from the heat. Pour into a heat-proof dish, cover with plastic wrap, and chill. The mix will thicken as it chills. Before serving, remove the cinnamon sticks and vanilla bean, sprinkle with the cinnamon-sugar, and decorate with the whipped cream.

MAKES 12 SERVINGS

BREAD PUDDING

Here is a good thing to do any time you have leftover bread or rolls. Biscuits can be used, too, but they will impart a baking powder taste to the pudding.

Pudding

1   cup sugar
12   large eggs
1   tablespoon vanilla extract
1   quart whole milk

Plumped raisins

½   cup raisins or any other dried fruit, diced if necessary
1   cinnamon stick
1   tablespoon firmly packed brown sugar
½   cup water
4   to 6 cups bread cubes
    Caramel sauce, for serving (see page 186)

To make the pudding, whisk together the sugar, eggs, and vanilla. Add the milk and whisk to dissolve the sugar.

To plump the raisins, bring the raisins, cinnamon stick, brown sugar, and water to a boil. Turn off the heat and allow the raisins to steep. Drain well.

Preheat the oven to 350°F. Fill a large baking dish or stainless steel roasting pan with the stale bread cubes. Can be any kind of white or wheat bread, any sweet variety, cinnamon bread, Danish, etc. Sprinkle the bread with the raisins and pour in the milk mixture. Mix well so that all of the bread is soaked with the mix. Bake for about 1 hour or until the pudding is set and puffs up in the middle and a knife inserted comes out clean. Cut and scoop out portions of the pudding and serve on a plate with caramel sauce drizzled over the top.

MAKES 12 TO 16 SERVINGS

Note: If preferred, leave the raisins out of the pudding and offer them as a complementary dish.

CARAMEL SAUCE

This recipe makes a much larger quantity than necessary. However, it produces a better quality caramel in this quantity. Reserve the extra sauce for other things such as French toast, ice cream, or apple pie.

5	cups heavy cream
2	cinnamon sticks
½	vanilla bean, split and scraped, seeds reserved
2	cups sugar

In a heavy-bottom pan, heat the cream over medium-high heat. Add the cinnamon sticks and vanilla bean with the seeds. Bring to a full boil, turn off the heat, and allow the mixture to steep on the stove. Meanwhile, place the sugar in another heavy-bottom pot and add enough water to make a paste. Scrape down the sides of the pot and place over medium heat to dissolve the sugar. Increase the heat to medium-high and boil the sugar until it starts to caramelize. Swirl the pan carefully to keep the color even. When it is amber in color, using a whisk with a long handle, carefully whisk in one-quarter of the warm cream. This will boil up and create a lot of steam. Repeat until all the cream is incorporated. Reduce the heat and allow the mixture to reduce by one-third. Strain into a heat-proof container and serve warm.

MAKES 4 CUPS

ORANGE BLOSSOM SPECIAL

Named for an immensely popular country song that was in turned named for a train, this dessert can be made extra special by using freshly squeezed orange juice instead of canned.

1	(3-ounce) package orange gelatin
¾	cup cold water
4	eggs
1	(18 ¼-ounce) box lemon cake mix
¾	cup vegetable oil
1	cup confectioners' sugar
2	tablespoons orange juice

Preheat the oven to 350°F. Stir the gelatin into the cold water. Add the eggs and beat for 2 minutes. Add the cake mix and beat 1 minute longer. Add the oil and beat for 2 more minutes. Pour the batter into a greased Bundt pan and bake for 40 minutes, being careful not to overbake. Combine the confectioners' sugar and orange juice for a glaze. Drizzle the glaze over the cake while it is hot.

MAKES 12 TO 16 SERVINGS

LINZER COOKIES

Here's a fortuitous accident. It began as a recipe for cheesecake crust, but Alisa felt that it was too messy and crumbly for that. She turned it into a cookie recipe that is a fabulous showcase for the Loveless's homemade preserves.

1½	cups granulated sugar
3	cups unbleached all-purpose flour
	Zest of 1½ lemons
9½	ounces (2 sticks plus 3 squares of a stick) unsalted butter, cold and cut into cubes
3	egg yolks
2	ounces cold water
2	cups preserves of your choice
	Confectioners' sugar

Place the sugar, flour, and lemon zest in a bowl with a flat beater. Cut in the butter and mix until it resembles fine crumbs. Add the egg yolks and cold water and mix until it forms a soft dough. Chill completely (several hours) before rolling out. Allow the dough to soften slightly and roll out with lots of flour to prevent sticking. Preheat the oven to 375°F. Brush off the flour and cut into hearts. Cut an even number of cookies and cut a hole in the center of half of the cookies, using a mini cutter. Place the cookies on parchment-lined baking sheets and bake for 12 to 14 minutes or until golden around the edges. Cool completely.

To assemble, spread the bottom halves (without the cutout) with preserves of your choice. Sprinkle the confectioners' sugar over the tops (the ones with the cutouts) and place the tops over the preserves to form sandwiches.

MAKES 4 TO 5 DOZEN COOKIES

BROWNIES

This is a recipe for brownies that are cakey rather than fudgy. Coffee enriches the chocolate flavor.

½   *pound (2 sticks) unsalted butter*

4   *ounces unsweetened chocolate*

2   *cups sugar*

4   *large eggs*

1   *tablespoon fine-ground coffee grounds*

1   *teaspoon vanilla extract*

1⅓ *cups unbleached all-purpose flour*

2   *tablespoons cocoa powder*

½   *teaspoon baking powder*

⅓   *cup chocolate chips*

Place the butter and chocolate in a large glass mixing bowl and place it inside a pot of barely simmering water to melt the chocolate. (Make sure the bowl doesn't touch the water.) Whisk together the sugar, eggs, coffee grounds, and vanilla. Whisk the sugar-egg mixture into the chocolate and butter. Sift the flour, cocoa powder, and baking powder over the chocolate mix and fold in. Preheat the oven to 350°F. Fold the chocolate chips into the chocolate mix and pour the final mixture into a greased, paper-lined, 9 x 13-inch pan. Sprinkle a few extra chips on top. Bake for 30 minutes or until a toothpick comes out almost clean with a few crumbs clinging to it. Do not overcook. Chill completely to remove from the pan. Run a knife around the edge and turn out onto a tray. Peel off the paper and place another tray on top. Invert the trays. Remove the top tray and cut the brownies.

MAKES 2 DOZEN BROWNIES

GRAHAM CRACKER SQUARES

I remember my mother making Graham cracker squares on a rainy day," Tom says. "It is so easy that even we kids could do it."

2¼   *cups graham cracker crumbs*
1   *(6-ounce) package chocolate chips*
1   *(14-ounce) can sweetened condensed milk*
        Confectioners' sugar

Preheat the oven to 350°F. Combine the crumbs, chocolate chips, and milk. Mix well. Spread the batter in a greased 8 x 8-inch pan and bake for 35 minutes. Cut into squares while warm and sprinkle with the confectioners' sugar.

MAKES 16 SQUARES

CHESS SQUARES

There is no "chess" in chess squares or chess pie. Folklore says that this very basic and unbeatable combination of sugar, butter, and flour got its name because someone asked what kind of pie it was. The cook answered, "It's jes' pie." It's the quintessential church cookbook dessert recipe. There is no "Chess," it's chess pie.

½	cup plus 6 tablespoons softened butter
⅓	cup confectioners' sugar
½	cup all-purpose flour
1½	cups sugar
1	tablespoon yellow cornmeal
1	tablespoon vanilla extract
1	tablespoon white vinegar
3	eggs

Preheat the oven to 350°F. Beat the 6 tablespoons butter in a mixer bowl until light and fluffy. Stir in the confectioners' sugar and flour; mixture will be crumbly. Press the mixture into the bottom of a 9-inch square baking pan. Bake for 20 minutes or until light brown. Combine the ½ cup butter and sugar in a mixing bowl until light and fluffy. Stir in the cornmeal, vanilla, and vinegar. Add the eggs 1 at a time, mixing well after each addition. Pour over the baked layer. Bake for 20 to 25 minutes or until the filling is almost set. Let stand until cool. Cut into squares.

MAKES 16 SERVINGS

TURTLE SQUARES

Turtle squares are the kind of sweet, gooey treat you find in church cookbooks everywhere. Squares like these are a classic 1950s treat for parties, lunch boxes, and TV snacks.

1	package 2-layer, German chocolate cake mix
1	(16-ounce) package caramels
½	cup (1 stick) butter
1	(6-ounce) can evaporated milk
2	cups chocolate chips

Preheat the oven to 350°F. Prepare the cake mix batter following the package directions. Pour half of the batter into a nonstick 9 x 13-inch baking pan. Bake for 15 minutes. Combine the caramels, butter, and evaporated milk in a saucepan. Cook over low heat until thick and creamy, stirring constantly. Pour over the baked layer. Sprinkle with chocolate chips. Pour the remaining cake batter over the top. Bake for 20 minutes longer. Let stand until cool. Cut into squares.

MAKES 18 SERVINGS

SNICKERDOODLES

Snickerdoodles are a can't-stop-eating-them cookie that are a classic, old-fashioned treat well-suited for parties, lunch boxes, and snacks any time of day.

½	cup shortening
1½	cups sugar
2	eggs
2¾	cups sifted all-purpose flour
2	teaspoons cream of tartar
1	teaspoon baking soda
¼	teaspoon sugar
2	teaspoons ground cinnamon

Preheat the oven to 400°F. Combine the shortening, sugar, and eggs in a mixing bowl; mix well. Combine the sifted flour, cream of tartar, and baking soda and add to the shortening mixture. Mix well. Shape the dough into 1-inch balls. Combine the sugar and cinnamon and roll the balls in the cinnamon-sugar. Arrange the balls 2 inches apart on an ungreased cookie sheet. Bake for 8 to 10 minutes or until light brown.

MAKES 3 DOZEN

JAM BARS

I always used to bake jam bars when I had my own bakery," Alisa said. "These are great for the Hams & Jams market because they are something people can grab and go. With our fresh homemade preserves, this is a natural. I mainly make strawberry and peach. Blackberry doesn't seem to appeal as much to people, probably because of the seeds in the berries."

1	cup rolled oats (not quick-cooking oats)
1½	cups unbleached all-purpose flour
1	cup firmly packed brown sugar
1	teaspoon ground cinnamon
½	teaspoon baking soda
½	cup chopped pecans
½	pound cold, unsalted butter, cut into cubes
¾	cup preserves

Preheat the oven to 375°F. Combine the oats, flour, brown sugar, cinnamon, baking soda, and pecans in a mixer bowl with a flat beater. Cut in the butter and mix until it forms crumbs. Reserve 1½ cups of this mix. Press the remaining mix into a greased, paper-lined, 9 x 13-inch pan. Bake for 20 minutes or until golden. When done, spread the preserves over the crust. Top with the reserved crumbs and return to the oven. Bake until the top is golden, about 20 minutes. Cool completely before removing from pan and cutting.

MAKES 2 DOZEN BARS

CHOCOLATE BISCUIT PUDDING

What do you do when you have leftover biscuits? Make chocolate biscuit pudding, which is like bread pudding with a cocoa kick.

8	small biscuits
2	cups milk
3	tablespoons cocoa
1	cup sugar
½	cup (1 stick) butter
2	eggs
1	tablespoon vanilla extract

Butter an 8 x 8-inch pan and preheat the oven to 400°F. Soak the biscuits in the milk for about 5 minutes or until soft. Add the cocoa, sugar, butter, eggs, and vanilla and mix together. Pour the biscuit mixture into the prepared pan and bake for 30 minutes.

MAKES 4 TO 6 SERVINGS

CARAMEL FILLING

½	cup buttermilk
¼	teaspoon baking soda
¼	cup tightly packed brown sugar
1	cup sugar
¼	cup (½ stick) butter
½	tablespoon vanilla extract

Combine the buttermilk, baking soda, brown sugar, sugar, and butter in a saucepan. Cook over medium heat until the mixture forms a soft ball. Let stand until cool. Stir in the vanilla. Pour into mixing bowl and beat until creamy.

MAKES 1 CUP

CARAMEL PIE

According to Tom, there is much confusion over the pronunciation of the word as two-syllable "carmel" with a soft "A" at the beginning or three syllable "caramel" with a harder "A." He says, "I don't know which is the true Southern way, but I suspect that if you leave out the middle A, you are a true southerner, and only you can judge the quality of this pie."

1	to 2 (8-ounce) cans sweetened condensed milk
1	baked (9-inch) pie shell or 8 small tart shells
	Cool Whip or unsweetened whipping cream (pint)

Pour the condensed milk into the top of a double boiler. Cover and boil for at least 1 hour. Pour the caramel into the baked pie shell or tart shells. Top with whipped cream or Cool Whip.

MAKES 8 SERVINGS

Natchez Trace

Long before Choctaw and Chickasaw Indians began using it as a convenient north-south hunting and travel route, long portions of the Natchez Trace were a favored trail for game. With its northern terminus just yards from where the Loveless Cafe is today (and where great salt licks once were a vital destination), one of America's oldest roads extends south from Central Tennessee 444 miles to Natchez, Mississippi. Early in the nineteenth century, farmers and trappers from Kentucky navigated down the Mississippi River to New Orleans to sell their goods in the spring. When business was finished, they sold or abandoned their flatboats then traveled the old wilderness route as a horse trail or footpath for their trip back north in the summer.

At that time, the path was known as the Boatman's Trail, and it was notorious for piracy and murders. After all, many of the farmers who used it were returning with skins full of gold from their sales, making them lucrative targets for highwaymen. The bandits' treachery was legend; they are said to have butchered their prey, weighed them down with rocks, and then sunk their bodies in obscure creeks.

All along the route, stands and primitive wayside inns were established to offer supplies and possible safe haven to travelers, and it was at one of these—Grinder's Stand about halfway between Nashville and the Alabama state line—that Meriwether Lewis, then governor of the territory of Louisiana, was found dead in 1809. The death of Lewis, best known as co-leader of the Lewis and Clark Expedition, was reported to President Jefferson as a suicide, but some historians believe he was murdered.

During the War of 1812, Andrew Jackson marched to New Orleans on the Natchez Trace, but by mid-century, the ascendance of steamboat travel along the Mississippi had made it a less vital trade trail. In 1938, President Roosevelt signed a measure creating the Natchez Trace Parkway, to be administered by the National Park Service. It is the seventh most visited national park with over thirteen million visits in 2003. Now part of the National Scenic Byways Program, the Parkway offers a wonderful opportunity for a curving, leisurely drive through sheltering canopies of trees and into American frontier history.

APPLESAUCE PIE

A cupboard shortcut, Tom explains, for those days when "you crave apple pie but don't have any apples."

1	(12-ounce) jar applesauce
½	cup plus 3 tablespoons sugar (or to taste)
1	teaspoon vanilla extract
½	cup (1 stick) butter
2	(9-inch) pie shells (see page 172)
3	tablespoons all-purpose flour

Preheat the oven to 375°F. In a large mixing bowl combine the applesauce, the ½ cup sugar, and vanilla. Cut the butter into the mixture and stir to combine. Place one pie shell in a 9-inch pie pan. Combine the flour and the remaining 3 tablespoons sugar and sprinkle over the pie shell. Pour in the applesauce mixture. Place the other pie shell on top and seal the edges with a fork. Make four slits in the top pie shell. Bake for 30 minutes or until golden brown.

MAKES 6 TO 8 SERVINGS

PEACH CUSTARD PIE

Peach has such a short life once it's harvested, you want to use it in as many ways as possible. The Loveless is most famous for its preserves, but this utterly simple—and utterly delicious—pie is a stellar dessert.

6	to 8 large peaches
1	unbaked (9-inch) pie shell (see page 172)
3	eggs
1	cup sugar
	Pinch of salt

Preheat the oven to 400°F. Peel the peaches and cut into large slices. Place the peaches in the pie shell. Beat the eggs, sugar, and salt together and pour the mix over the peaches. Bake for 15 minutes. Reduce the heat to 325°F and continue baking for another 45 minutes. Serve warm or cool.

MAKES 6 TO 8 SERVINGS

RED VELVET CAKE

I once bought a farm from a lady in east Tennessee," Tom recalls. "Before we signed the contract, she insisted we sit down for a piece of her red velvet cake. She used butter in her recipe, and it was unbelievably rich, so much so that I drank three glasses of milk with my one little slice. Red velvet cake is a Southern tradition that goes way back."

1½	cups sugar
1½	cups canola oil
2	eggs
1	teaspoon vanilla extract
2½	cups cake flour
1	tablespoon cocoa powder
1	teaspoon baking soda
1	cup buttermilk
2	ounces red food color (1 small bottle)
1	teaspoon white vinegar

Grease two 9-inch cake pans. Preheat the oven to 350°F. Whisk the sugar, oil, eggs, and vanilla together in a bowl. Sift the flour, cocoa powder, and baking soda over the egg mixture. Add the buttermilk and stir to combine. Add the food color and vinegar and stir. Pour the batter into the prepared cake pans and bake for about 30 minutes or until a toothpick inserted into the center comes out clean. Let the cake cool completely before frosting. Use the cream cheese frosting recipe on page 164.

MAKES 2 CAKES, 10 TO 12 SERVINGS

CHOCOLATE ZUCCHINI CAKE

Tom describes this ultra moist cake as "Our way of letting the chocolate lover fool himself into thinking he is eating something healthy."

1	cup (2 sticks) unsalted butter, softened
1¾	cups sugar
2	eggs
1	teaspoon vanilla extract
2½	cups unbleached all-purpose flour
4	tablespoons cocoa powder
1½	teaspoons baking powder
1	teaspoon baking soda
1	teaspoon ground cinnamon
½	teaspoon ground cloves
½	cup buttermilk
2	cups grated zucchini
½	cup mini chocolate chips

Grease a tube pan and sprinkle with flour. Preheat the oven to 350°F. Cream the butter and sugar together in a large bowl. Add the eggs and vanilla and beat to combine. Sift together the flour, cocoa powder, baking powder, baking soda, cinnamon, and cloves. Add the buttermilk and grated zucchini to the egg mixture alternately with the dry ingredients. Fold in the chocolate chips. Pour the batter into the tube pan. Bake for about 55 minutes or until a toothpick inserted into the center comes out clean.

MAKES 1 CAKE, 6 TO 8 SERVINGS

OATMEAL COOKIES

Alisa refers to this as "the best oatmeal cookie recipe there is." Sorghum or molasses works as a sweetener, and they can include raisins, currants, dried cranberries, even chocolate chips.

1	cup (2 sticks) unsalted butter, softened
2	cups sugar
3	tablespoons molasses or sorghum
1	teaspoon vanilla extract
2	eggs
3	cups rolled oats (not instant)
2½	cups all-purpose flour
2	teaspoons baking soda
1	teaspoon ground cinnamon
1	to 1½ cups raisins (or currants or dried cranberries)

Preheat the oven to 375°F. Cream the butter, sugar, molasses or sorghum, and vanilla together in a bowl. Add the eggs and mix well. Add the oats, flour, baking soda, and cinnamon and mix well. Add the raisins and mix. Arrange mounds of dough (1 heaping tablespoon to ⅓ cup in size) on a cookie sheet and bake for 7 to 15 minutes or until the cookies are brown around the edges and no longer glossy on top. The cooking time will depend on the size of the cookies.

MAKES 1 TO 2 DOZEN COOKIES

Index

Numbers in italics refer to pages with illustrations